Clay Aiken

From Second Place to the Top of the Charts

KATHLEEN TRACY

PO Box 196 • Hockessin, Delaware 19707 •
www.mitchelllane.com

Mitchell Lane
PUBLISHERS

Mitchell Lane
PUBLISHERS

Printing 1 2 3 4 5

ISBN 1-58415-326-1

PUBLISHER'S NOTE: This book is an UNAUTHORIZED biography of Clay Aiken. No part of this book has been endorsed nor authorized by Clay Aiken or any person representing Clay Aiken. The author and publisher have no affiliation with *American Idol* nor any of its producers or contestants.

This book has been thoroughly researched and to the best of our knowledge represents a true story. While every possible effort has been made to ensure accuracy, the publisher will not assume liability for damages caused by inaccuracies in the data, and makes no warranty on the accuracy of the information contained herein. Should anyone know of any inaccuracies in this story, please email corrections to mitchelllane@mitchelllane.com so corrections can be made in a future edition. The publisher maintains its right as independent media to publish this book.

The internet sites referenced in this book were all active as of the publication date. The publisher cannot guarantee they will all be working at the time you are reading this book.

The publisher supports Clay Aiken's desire to capitalize on his new celebrity for the benefit of children with disabilities. To that end, a portion of the proceeds from the sale of this book benefit the Bubel/Aiken Foundation.

Table of Contents

Introduction

If you can dream it, you can be it.

As children, we all believe we can be anything we set our minds to, from doctor to astronaut to president of the United States. But unfortunately as we get older, we sometimes lose faith in ourselves, especially when it seems the odds are against us. Rather than risk failure, we stop pursuing our dreams and give up the opportunity to see what might happen.

Clay Aiken has proved to millions of fans the world over why we should never stop believing in ourselves and in our dreams. Against incredible odds, Clay went from living a quiet life in North Carolina as a special education teacher candidate to international singing fame simply because he had the courage to take a chance.

Although his vocal talent is what initially attracted fans, Clay's appeal goes much deeper than that. Having to overcome a difficult childhood grounded Clay, and his down-to-earth demeanor is a refreshing reminder that success can be enjoyed and embraced with disarming humility and heartfelt graciousness and gratitude. His connection with and appreciation of his audience is genuine, and his uncompromising insistence to remain true to who he is—a moral man who believes celebrities have a responsibility to be role models—has turned Clay into much more than a pop star. To many he's become a hero, the underdog "nerd" who succeeded in becoming a true pop idol and who did so while keeping his ego firmly checked at the door.

It is often said that success doesn't really change you, it simply magnifies who you already are inside. For some, success becomes an excuse for diva behavior, grandiose expectations and self-indulgence. But in the case of Clay Aiken, fame means having a world stage on which he can entertain more people, better promote causes dear to his heart, and be a vibrant example, through both his actions and his music, that good things will come if you have faith in your dreams. And that is the true measure of this man.

Chapter One
We're Not in Kansas Anymore

Despite the stifling heat, the over six thousand people who were packed into the Universal Amphitheater were buzzing with anticipation. It was Wednesday, May 21, 2003, and the second-season finale of *American Idol* was about to begin. Uncertainty abounded, because this year's contest was too close to call. The only thing anyone knew was that the voting was going to be tight and that the fans of whoever lost would surely feel robbed. Unlike the previous year, when Kelly Clarkson was the obvious pick of the talent litter going into the final, this time America—as well as the *American Idol* judges—seemed evenly split over whether the winner should be Birmingham, Alabama's Ruben "the Velvet Teddy Bear" Studdard or the boy next door with the golden voice, Clay Aiken, the pride of Raleigh, North Carolina.

Backstage, Ruben and Clay distracted themselves from the mounting pressure by joking with each other and the rest of the Top 12 finalists who would perform during the telecast. Although only Aiken and Studdard were vying for the *American Idol* title, because this was Hollywood, even runners-up would be showered with surprises.

Waiting backstage for all the finalists were lavish gifts provided by top-shelf companies eager to be associated with the *American Idol* phenomenon. Lois Hill Accessories brought an assortment of jewelry, including bracelets and necklaces; the Shoreham Hotel offered a weekend stay at their posh Manhattan digs; the newest digital toy, XM Satellite Radio, caught Rickey Smith's fancy; while others were impressed with leather goods from designer Donald J. Pliner. Clay posed for some photos, holding up a video explaining the wonders of Lasik eye surgery, before going off by himself. He wanted to collect his thoughts prior to the start of the special two-hour finale.

Out on stage, *American Idol*'s co-executive producer, Nigel Lythgoe, prepped the audience to raise the energy level even higher. "Who's for Clay?" he shouted. The resulting applause and screams were almost deafening. "Who's for Ruben?" he asked, and the floor of the amphitheater shook from the noise.

The first part of the telecast was basically a sixty-minute tease for an audience craving to see Ruben and Clay. Among the segments shown was a clip reel of lowlights from various international *Idol* shows, showing some cringe-worthy performances from countries including France, England, Germany, and Lebanon. Arguably the least talented performance came from U.S. contestant Keith Beukelaer, whose rendition of Madonna's "Like a Virgin" caused Simon Cowell to snap that Keith had to be "the worst singer in the world."

By the time the second half of the show arrived, the audience was almost begging to hear the would-be Idols. They finally got their wish when Kelly Clarkson, the 2002 Idol, sang a medley with Ruben and Clay. They were joined by the other 2003 finalists, who sang another medley of songs made famous by the season's guest judges, including "Midnight Train to Georgia" and "Let's Get Physical." Kimberley Locke got her moment to shine when she joined Clay and Ruben for the songs "Superstar," "On the Wings of Love," and "Somewhere Over the Rainbow."

As the excitement rose, so did the temperature, with people openly fanning themselves. During one commercial break, producer Lythgoe begged the audience to "try and stop looking like you're too hot. Make yourselves look alive. Breathe!"

Throughout the evening, emcee Ryan Seacrest tantalized the audience with snippets of information on the voting results, revealing the tally from certain states. Not surprisingly, Ruben carried Alabama, while Clay won New York. But

Seacrest was serious when he said that the voting was the closest ever seen on *American Idol.* Out of 24 million votes cast, there was a difference of less than one percent between the winner and the runner-up.

It was down to just Clay and Ruben. They each reprised their performances from the previous night, with Clay crooning "Bridge Over Troubled Water" and Ruben singing "Flying Without Wings." Both performances almost caused the theater to implode from the sounds of wild cheering. People had come from all across America to root for their favorites in person, and the energy hummed through the audience.

Writer Michael Gross recounted in an MSN article how he had met one Clay Aiken fan by a souvenir stand. She had flown out from Michigan after her sister surprised her with tickets to the finale. According to Gross, "She held a big homemade poster that said, NORTHVILLE, MICHIGAN ❤ CLAY!! I asked, 'Did you come all the way out here just for this?' She wiped her eyes and took a deep breath. 'It's a lot more exciting to be here. You feel like you're a celebrity, too. Because we were screaming and he was mouthing *Thank you*. To us. Right to us. You feel like you're inside it.'"

Finally, the time for singing was over. The two friends joined Seacrest onstage. Stretching out the drama as long as possible, the three judges—Simon Cowell, Paula Abdul, and Randy Jackson—gave their final thoughts to Aiken and Studdard, all keeping true to form. Paula praised them both for their talent and made it clear she thought they were both winners. Jackson called the men his "dawgs," and Simon, the consummate businessman, revealed that Clay and Ruben would both be releasing singles on the same day, regardless of the outcome.

As he looked out at the audience, waiting to hear the results, Clay felt oddly calm. He had already come farther than he had ever imagined he could, having experienced so many amazing adventures, been overwhelmed by the support of fans all across the country, made close new friends, and grown so much as a person—whatever the final tally was, he later said, he truly felt as if he had already won. He turned to look at Ruben and Seacrest, thinking he really had traveled over the rainbow.

Chapter Two

Growing Up a Tar Heel

While everyone appreciates how much influence family life has on our personalities, where we grow up can also play an integral part in molding our individual attitudes and values. Clay Aiken would probably be just as talented and disarmingly charming regardless of where he'd been born, but growing up in the South undoubtedly helped instill humility, community, and faith, values he admittedly holds dear.

Although it might currently be most famous for being Clay Aiken's home state, North Carolina has been an important part of American history for over four centuries. Some of the earliest European settlers staked a claim in the New World in North Carolina, and in fact, it is where the first non-Indian American was born, a girl named Virginia Dare in 1587. It is also where the earliest "unsolved mystery" on North American soil occurred, on Roanoke Island off the Carolina coast. The story is one every local schoolchild knows.

In 1584, famous British adventurer Walter Raleigh sailed to the New World to claim land for England. After a three-month voyage, his expedition landed in present-day North Carolina. Raleigh spent a couple of months exploring and building a relationship with the local Native Americans. When he returned to England, the queen was so thrilled with his report that she knighted Raleigh and commissioned him to establish a fort and permanent military colony. After the first attempt failed, Raleigh led a third expedition that settled on Roanoke Island in 1587. Raleigh and his associates sailed back to England, leaving the settlers on their own.

Three years later when the island was revisited, the settlement was deserted. The houses were gone, the fields grown over. There was no sign of life. The only clue to the fate of the colonists was the word *Croatoan* carved in a tree, which referred to another island nearby. There was no sign of the settlers on that island, either. To this day, the mystery of Carolina's "lost colony" remains unsolved. The tragedy was so unnerving that it would be another seven years before England would make another attempt to establish a permanent colony in the New World, which they did successfully at Jamestown in 1607. It would be another hundred years after that before the Carolinas attracted thriving settlements. In 1788, the city of Raleigh, named after Sir Walter, was founded on a parcel of land bought from a local tavern owner and was built specifically to serve as the state capital.

From the city's beginning, the people of Raleigh have prided themselves on exuding Southern hospitality, on being a friendly, tight-knit community that promotes strong personal values and neighborly warmth. "It's a pretty big city," Clay said, "but it's got a very small-town feel. Everybody knows everybody."

There is also a deep appreciation of the arts among Raleighites. In 1943, North Carolina became the first state to provide financial support for an orchestra: the North Carolina Symphony. Based in Raleigh, the symphony performs over 150 concerts a year. In 1947, the North Carolina Museum of Art was established as the nation's first state-supported art museum.

So for a little boy with a penchant for music, Raleigh was a perfect place to grow up. Clayton Holmes Grissom was born there on November 30, 1978, and seemed destined for a musical life. His parents, Faye and Vernon, had fallen in love in part because of their shared passion for music. The couple had first met when they joined a band in the 1970s.

Wade Harris, a longtime friend of Grissom's, told *Star* magazine, "Vernon was an extraordinary singer/guitarist, and Faye was an excellent singer. They were both really talented.

The three of us, plus drummer Billy Winston, had a great local group back in the '70s called the Southland Band. There's no doubt about it, Clay picked up a lot of his ability from his dad and mom. Vernon could have been a star of the Grand Ole Opry—he was that good!" Vernon was especially partial to bluegrass music.

Despite her being eleven years younger, Faye was swept away by Vernon, who made his living as an automobile parts salesman. The couple married, but the honeymoon was short-lived. Life with Vernon, who drank a lot, was difficult for Faye, and the marriage quickly floundered. Just one week before Clay's first birthday, Faye packed a bag and left with her son. "I remember crying," she told Erik Hedegaard, "because Clayton wasn't at his home to have his birthday party, and I had made his birthday cake, and it was back in the freezer and it was just like, *I don't have my baby's birthday cake.*"

Not only had Vernon been an alcoholic, but Clay would eventually discover that his father had also been physically abusive to Faye, which explains her desperate attempts to find a safe place for her and Clay to live. "We kind of lived on the run," Clay later recounted in a *Rolling Stone* interview. "Actually, not on the run so much as we moved back and forth to stay away from him. We moved so he wouldn't know where I was."

Eventually, Faye and Vernon divorced, and Vernon was granted visitation rights with Clay. According to *Star,* Vernon Grissom, who had two older children from a previous marriage, missed his son. "Losing his little boy was deeply troubling for Vernon," commented an unnamed friend.

Although Clay seems to dismiss the possibility out of hand, Faye seems more thoughtful about the relationship Clay might have had with his father. As she observed in the interview with Hedegaard, "You know, his dad was a musician, so music was something they had in common. After their visits, I would say to Clayton, 'Well, did your dad get out the guitar and play guitar with you or anything?' And he would say, 'No, Dad never did. He was always sick.' And, well, I think as he got older, he understood what that sick was. They say that blood is thicker than water. But sometimes it is not."

Like many children of alcoholics, young Clay had to endure undeserved emotional hurts. The worst time, he told ABC News' Diane Sawyer, was when "he said I was a mistake." Aiken also admitted his father's abuse was something he and his mother really don't discuss. "She doesn't talk about it—ever. And I don't know how thrilled she is of me talking about it either. There are pictures of what he did to her. So, you know, I know it's true."

Even through all the ugliness, Clay seemed willing to try to establish some kind of relationship with Vernon, but Grissom was either unwilling or unable to make the effort. Aiken recalls as a teenager telling Vernon he needed to try harder. "I just said, 'You don't ever call me and ask me to come. I always call you. Next time you want to see me, give me a call and I'll drive up.'" Although Vernon responded, "Sure thing," Clay says, "He never called. Ever."

Clay, who usually refers to Vernon by his first name and designates him merely as a "sperm donor," told *Rolling Stone* he did learn valuable lessons from watching his father. "I think I learned to be who I am by being everything he wasn't. Part of the reason I don't smoke is that he did. He drank, and I don't. He's a racist, and I'm not. I don't want anything to do with any of that."

Fortunately for Clay, when he was six, his mom fell in love with and married Ray Parker, a gentle man whom Aiken calls "the only dad I ever had." While Ray might not have had Vernon's musical skills, he was still Clay's number one supporter when it came to singing. And according to Faye, Clay was singing almost as soon as he could talk. When he was sixteen months old, Faye said, Clay would sing along to country songs playing on the radio, including in her car as they drove around.

Faye told Leigh Dyer of the *Charlotte Observer,* "The first song I remember him singing was 'Mama, Don't Let Your Babies Grow Up to Be Cowboys.' I knew he had something special. I knew God gave him a great voice."

Performing seemed to be as much in his blood as his red hair. Faye worked at Sears as an in-house interior designer, and on occasion she would take Clay to work with her. "The people there loved him," she recalled to Erik Hedegaard. "They'd put him up on the counters and say, 'I'll give you a dollar to sing.' Sometimes they'd even pay him five dollars." Occasionally Clay would add a little acting to his performance, claiming he wouldn't sing because he was too tired. But then he would go over to his mom and ask her to wind him up. "So we'd pretend to wind him up like a little toy box, and off he'd go, singing again."

In an interview with Fred Bronson, Clay said he enjoyed the attention. "It wasn't that I could sing really well. It was just that I would do it. Some kids are shy and I was never very shy. So it was not, 'Oh, he's so talented at three years old.' It was just, 'He'll make a fool of himself on the carpet samples, so let's let him do it.' At five, I had shown that I could stay on pitch."

So at that age, Aiken auditioned to perform at a high school winter dance, which had a tradition of having a mascot sing at the event. At the audition, Clay sang "Islands in the Stream," a song he had gotten to know from listening to the radio with his mom. Faye recalled, "The students laughed so hard he stopped singing." Aiken told columnist Fred Bronson he remembers turning to his mom and saying, "They're laughing at me, and she said, 'No, they think you're cute.'" And she was right—Clay was selected as mascot. But Clay is quick to point out that he never felt pressured into performing. "My mom supported me in doing that type of thing," he stressed in an *Entertainment Weekly* interview. "She was never a stage mommy, just drove me to things, and if somebody needed help to fundraise, she'd work the ticket booth."

Clay's first cousin Karen Santos affectionately recalled to the *Virginian-Pilot* that when he was six years old, Clay sometimes resembled Howdy Doody, but what she remembered most was his voice. "I remember the first time I saw Clay sing. He was standing in my mother's den. My uncle Ray Parker had married Clay's mom, Faye Aiken, and they were visiting from Raleigh. My uncle barked at Clay, 'Sing a song, boy.' Without missing a beat, Clay opened his little mouth and belted one out. Even then, I was amazed by his talent."

It seems everyone in his family believed Clay had been born with a special gift. His grandmother, Catherine Aiken, recalled watching Clay play in her backyard as a boy. "When he was little, he was real thoughtful," Catherine told the Raleigh area newspaper, the *Herald-Sun*. "He never has liked sports. And he would come out here and his granddaddy would have a swing out there in the backyard. And he'd sit out there and swing and sing. Almost when he started talking, he started singing."

One of the things Clay loved doing was listening to music in his room on his little plastic Fisher-Price turntable. He loved it so much that when he was seven he decided to respond to a music club ad he saw in a magazine. "I saw one of those magazines that said 'twelve for the price of one,'" Clay recalled in a *Billboard* interview. "Back then they were LPs. I don't know how I was smart enough at seven years old to put it in the mail and order the twelve." Aiken says he doesn't remember everything he ordered. "I remember getting the Crystal Gayle album and then Marie Osmond sang a duet with Dan Seals, 'Meet Me in Montana.' I remember that song." Faye was not amused at her son's initiative. "My mom was furious with the company for allowing a seven-year-old to do that. But all I had to do was tape a penny to that little piece of cardboard and send it in."

Once he was in a stable home with two working, loving parents, Clay thrived. According to the city Web site, Raleigh is known as the City of Oaks and often is described as "a park with a city in it." Clay's neighborhood was no exception, with tree-lined streets and comfortable homes. Although Faye and Ray were nurturing, they were also strict. Clay knew if he were ever rude or if he cursed, he'd get his mouth washed out with soap. Bad behavior might result in a spanking with a switch from a tree. But the times Faye had to discipline Clay were rare, and although he was exuberant, he managed to stay out of trouble.

Music gave Clay a direction and someplace he could belong. But for as much as he loved singing, he was less enthusiastic about studying it formally. "I took piano lessons for about four months, and that was too much," he told *Billboard.* "And then I took singing lessons for about two months and that was too much." When it came to singing for the pure joy of it, though, Aiken sang whenever and wherever he could.

Former schoolmate Alisha Puckett says being friends with Clay was like living in a Hollywood musical. "In yearbook class, in the middle of conversations, in the middle of lunch and even in the middle of lecture, Clay would break out into song. He had a voice, as we all know, and he loved to practice for anyone who would listen."

At his mother's urging, Clay sang at Leesville Road Baptist Church. Frances Wilson remembers the first time she heard Clay singing there. "He blew me away, this tiny little boy with red hair and wire-rimmed glasses and a bow tie—and that incredible voice." Years later, when he was seventeen, Clay won a country music singing contest, and afterward he began performing at various community shows. Frances would perform with him as "Auntie Frances." They also incorporated comedy skits, such as Auntie Frances shoving a chocolate cake in her face.

As a youngster, Clay joined the Raleigh Boychoir, which has become a respected institution in the city. As Aiken admitted to *Billboard,* "It was not the type of music I liked but it let me sing."

According to the organization's Web site, the boychoir was founded in 1968 so that boys between eight and fifteen years old—whose voices have not yet changed from puberty—can have the opportunity to learn about choral music and to perform in front of audiences at a variety of public concerts. But beyond learning about music, according to the Web site, the goal of the boychoir, and of founder Thomas E. Sibley, is to help mold better young men, providing each boy "with a rich, unique, and unforgettable experience which will remain an integral part of him throughout his life. Through the musical training and choral experiences, he develops an appreciation of a wide range of choral literature. He gains self-confidence and poise. He learns how to meet demands—musical and otherwise. He learns how to be a leader as well as how to be a worker in a closely integrated group. He acquires self-discipline and self-respect. He knows that what he does is of real musical excellence as well as knowing that what he does is contributing to the community through the arts."

In the seventh grade, Clay also became a member of his school choir—even though at Leesville Road Middle School, he was the only boy among forty girls in the choral group and would be positioned in the front center. Puckett said Clay always "looked like he was having fun. Clay had the most recognizable voice." The *Collegiate Standard,* a journal for North Carolina's colleges and universities, quotes a girl named Cara who went to the same summer camp Clay did. "I can remember all of the talent shows at summer camp where I would wait all summer just to hear the sound of Clay's voice."

One reason Clay felt so comfortable singing was that he knew he could carry a tune. "At the risk of sounding cocky, I always knew I could sing," he admitted in a PBS Kids interview, but he added that his willingness to perform had more to do with his personality than any innate talent. "A kid that will jump up and sing at that age, it's not that they're good, it's just that they're outgoing enough to do it. It was probably eighth grade when I realized, when people started telling me."

Clay also enjoyed school. Puckett remembered Clay as the life of the classroom party. "Clayton was busy masterminding jokes and witty remarks, which he conjured up with great ease," she wrote in the *Herald-Sun,* recalling when she was in seventh grade and Clay was a year ahead of her and they were both in the yearbook class. "He was one of Leesville Road Middle School's class clowns. Often sarcastic, often theatrical, borderline annoying.

"Of course, his hair wasn't like that when I knew him, and his eyes weren't as easy to see under his inch-thick eyeglasses, rimmed with bright gold." Alisha also recalled that his hair was never out of place, and his fashion sense was definitely his own. For example, he was fond of wearing plaid shorts. "His clothes were never trendy. He loved to wear jackets—it didn't matter if it was raining or cold," she wrote.

Although as a kid Clay had a circle of friends, he recalled feeling more comfortable with grown-ups. "I was more sociable with adults," he said in a *Launch Radio* interview. "I was with my mom and her friends, and I didn't go off to play that often. It was just my mother and me until I was six, and then I automatically got a brother and a sister when she got married. There was a big gap in age." Ray's kids, Jeff and Amy, were, respectively, nine and six years older than Clay.

Despite his eccentric appearance, Clay said he didn't get picked on. "I don't think I gave anybody a reason to bully me. The thing about bullies is if you show them that you're intimidated and you're upset by them, they're gonna keep doing it. I'd be, 'Forget you, then,' and walk away. I don't let things get under my skin as much as some people do."

Although Clay was always outgoing, by the time he entered high school, the teenager was going through a typical period of adolescent insecurity, unsure of himself and concerned about whether or not he fit in. But as always, music would eventually show him the way.

Chapter Three
Coming of Age

Everybody wants to fit in and to be liked and accepted for who they are. But never does it seem more important than during high school. For many people, their high school experience seems to leave an indelible mark that forever informs their lives. Since high school, and everything wonderful and stressful about it, is an experience that almost every person in the United States shares, Clay's angst and insecurity is immediately relatable.

Clay's mom told writer Maryann B. Hunsberger that as her son got older, he became more self-conscious. Even though computer geeks-turned-billionaires like Bill Gates and Steve Jobs have made nerdiness almost fashionable among Baby Boomers, among teenagers, any skinny kid who wears thick glasses and is more comfortable singing in the choir than playing on the football field is bound to be a target for teasing. Faye said Clay "would get upset because the football guys in middle school would pick on him. I said, 'One day, they're not going to be playing football, but you'll still have your voice.'" She said he eventually found his niche and "became quite popular in high school."

Clay told *Teen People* that during his tween years in middle school, "I was confident. I was the big mouth of the class, and I thought I knew everything. Eighth and ninth grade were my big problem times. You know when your parents try to say something cool or when you had an old teacher who tried to use the lingo and it just didn't sound right? Everyone else can say 'phat' and it's cool, but when your teacher said it you were like, 'What?!' That is how I was in eighth and ninth grade. I was trying, but I was not pulling it off."

Clay is well aware his eclectic fashion sense didn't help. "The first two years of high school, I was shy," he told *Cosmo Girl*. "I got picked on for the way I dressed: I had Coke-bottle glasses, and my hair was always just atrocious." Aiken joked to *Entertainment Weekly*, "I actually started convincing myself that wedgies were compliments. My friends used to give me wedgies, and I would convince people that that's what they did because they were friends of mine."

Then when he was a sophomore, Clay experienced a personal epiphany. "I just decided I was going to be myself. I still wasn't the coolest person in school, but I was happier with myself and I had confidence and I started to become more popular. By twelfth grade I was set. I still looked the same—I still looked kind of dorky—but I was totally in. I was popular; it was how I carried myself. I got more confident with who I was. I just realized, I'm never gonna be a Brad Pitt, so get over it, be happy with yourself, and move on. People feel comfortable around someone who is comfortable with himself."

Clay feels so strongly about the importance of being happy and accepting of who you are that he agreed to write a foreword for the book *Yes, Your Parents Are Crazy!* In it he says, "Being a teenager can be hard sometimes. Not long ago, I struggled with the same problems you do and felt the same things you feel. I was the nice, kind of nerdy, average kid who sits next to you in school. I wanted to be cool and to fit in, but I never really felt good about myself—how I looked, how I dressed—all the stuff that seems really important to you. Now I understand that my clothes and my 'look' are just the 'wrapping,' what's on the *outside*. What really counts is what's *inside* of me—who I am, what I believe in.

"When I was about 17, I finally decided that it was just too much work to try to be what other kids thought was acceptable, and I decided to be who I am—nothing more, nothing less. That's when everything changed. I was finally able to focus on what's important to *me*. I still wasn't the coolest kid in school, but it gave me the confidence to open up to more people and become more outgoing. The more comfortable I was with myself, the more comfortable other people were with me. For the first time, I felt really good about *myself*."

When asked to describe himself as a teenager, Clay told *Rolling Stone* he was "bubbly" while performing or speaking in front of groups or reading the morning announcements over the school loudspeaker. But among his classmates, he was more contained. "In my circle, I wasn't Ferris Bueller," he said. "I was Ferris Bueller's friend." And he adopted the attitude, "There's nothing so wrong that it can't be easily fixed or easily ignored. I just let things roll off."

Once Clay made the decision to embrace who he was, he was fearless in his individuality. One of his friends at Leesville Road High School, Amanda Ward, remembers Clay as "the life of every party. You never knew what color hair Clayton was going to have," she told the *Herald-Sun*. "He always dyed his hair. You never knew what he was going to wear. He had these bright green tennis shoes, just crazy clothes," including a pair of yellow high-tops.

His choice of pet was equally eclectic. "He had a pet goat that he would bring around," Amanda recalled. "It was a miniature goat named Zoe. Most people would have pet dogs, I just remember he had this pet goat. He would bring it everywhere he went. He would take it to my house. He walked it on a leash, and it was the craziest thing in the world. It wasn't that crazy coming from him because we expected things like that."

Geoffrey Graybeal, one of Aiken's closest friends in middle and high school, remembers Clay being fun—and responsible. He recalled that after he was old enough to get his driver's license, Clay was always the designated driver for both close friends and general acquaintances after parties.

In an interview with radio station Mix 96 in Tulsa, Faye recalled, "He was the typical kid growing up, but I did not have to worry about him getting into trouble. Clayton was never a party person, so I did not have to worry about the driving and drinking. Many times he would get out of bed at night to go pick up a friend that had called who did not feel could drive himself home. Clayton would leave me a note in case I woke to say that he had to pick up someone and he would never say who. Believe it or not, what you see with him is what you get—he has lots of compassion for other people, especially those with social neglects."

In high school, Clay continued to pursue music. Geoffrey Graybeal told the *Herald-Sun* he remembered the time Clay performed the national anthem at Raleigh's Dorton Arena for the city's minor league hockey team, the Raleigh Ice Caps (who have since relocated to Augusta, Georgia). His dad, Ray, was still Clay's number one fan and encouraged him to join his brother's country band. Clay also started dabbling in acting. "When I was in high school, choir wasn't enough, so I did some musicals." The school productions included *Oklahoma!* and *The Music Man,* in which Clay said he played one of the councilmen.

One summer, Clay performed with the Raleigh Little Theatre. Founded in 1936, the theater is one of the oldest continuously operating community theaters in the country. Clay appeared in RLT's dinner theater production of *The Sound of Music.* Also in that production was Frankie Muniz, who would go on to star in *Malcolm in the Middle.* Clay admits theater was hard work, but he reveled in performing for an audience and being bathed in their applause.

Of course, the production Clay remembers most vividly is the one in which he wasn't involved. "I did the freshman, sophomore and junior plays," he said in a *Charlotte Observer* interview. "In twelfth grade, we did *Guys and Dolls* and I got cut; didn't get a part at all. Didn't even get in the chorus. My music teacher was not the nicest lady." Clay explained he felt he was the victim of payback by the teacher.

"Wake County schools have an annual showcase of arts and they had 300 acts audition and I had asked her for years if I could do it. And she said, 'Well, your senior year you can audition as a soloist.' She changed her mind my senior year and I decided to do it anyway. I got someone else to sponsor me and I did a solo. It was the biggest audience I'd ever sung in front of at the time. I think it was like 2,000 people in this Memorial Auditorium downtown and I sang 'This Is the Moment' from *Jekyll and Hyde*. I made it and her choir did not, so I'd say she was bitter."

But by and large, Aiken's teachers remember him fondly. His high school principal, Mr. Murphy, described him to *Rolling Stone* with glowing accolades. "He was absolutely a gift. A gift."

Another of his teachers, Elsie Norton, who was Clay's chorus instructor at Leesville Road Middle School, told writer Cle Pickett, "Clay was very dedicated. He was always there when I needed him. If anyone was going to audition for a solo, if he was auditioning, they usually probably didn't audition because they knew he'd probably get the part." Clay's later fame would also make Ms. Norton, who is now director of choral music at Southeast Raleigh High School, a local celebrity as the teacher who nurtured the boy who went on to be a pop star. "When I found out I was going to Southeast I was like, 'Oh my God, I'm going to be taught by the same teacher as Clay Aiken was,'" gushed Ashleigh Hocutt to Pickett. "I'm really thrilled that I could be a student of Ms. Norton."

While some teachers nurtured him musically, others inspired him to consider following another path. "There were two teachers, Miss Propes and Miss Stone, who were very good and in tune with high school kids," Aiken told PBS Kids. "They had an ability to get passionate about whatever the students were passionate about and they made me want to be a teacher."

Clay would later remind teens that a lot can be learned by watching and listening to the adults in their lives. "So much of what helped me get through those tough times came from good adults around me. Yes, parents can be annoying, even 'crazy,' and yes, teachers can be boring. But the truth is that those annoying, boring adults can help you a lot, if you can somehow learn how to talk and listen to each other—I mean *really* talk, and *really* listen," he wrote in the foreword to *Yes, Your Parents Are Crazy!*

After he graduated from high school, Clay knew he had some decisions to make. In an interview for *EP Magazine,* at eparent.com, he noted, "Every time I'd do a play, I said, 'This is what I want to do for the rest of my life.' Every time I'd sing in choir, 'This is what I want to do for the rest of my life.' And then I got out of high school and I realized, 'I don't think this is what I want to do.' I thought about going to school for music and I said, 'No, I'm not sure that I want to be a musician.' I'm so not big on instability and I did not want to knock on doors for the rest of my life and hope somebody would hear me."

Aiken at various times also toyed with the idea of being a journalist or a politician, although neither felt like the perfect fit. So, thinking back to those teachers who had made such an impression on him, Clay began searching for his calling in life.

Chapter Four

College Daze

Even as a teenager, Clay had a way with younger children. When he was at Leesville Road Middle School, he was recruited to spend an hour a day to help teach gym class to elementary school students. He seemed to have an innate understanding and empathy with kids and a genuine affection for them. During high school, that led him to work at a summer day camp program held at Raleigh's Brentwood Elementary School and after school as a camp counselor at the A.E. Finley YMCA. At the camp, he particularly enjoyed spending time and working with children suffering from autism, a childhood affliction characterized by emotional withdrawal, language disorders, and the inability to form normal social relationships. It takes great patience to work with kids who are autistic because it can often be very frustrating, but Clay was never ruffled.

Suzanne Lyczkowski was also a counselor at the Y. She told the *Herald-Sun* that Clay would do anything for the kids he worked with. "He was definitely one of the favorite counselors," she recalled. "If he asked them to do anything, they would do it because they just loved him."

She also said Aiken's biggest accomplishment was convincing the children to treat each other with respect. "Every summer, he would do a gender competition with his kids," she said. "Who could be nicer to each other, and at the end of the week he would let the kindest group duct tape him to the wall."

Jeff Flake, one of the YMCA supervisors, said some of Clay's accomplishments bordered on the miraculous. "I have witnessed him take a child with autism who couldn't communicate, and by the end of the school year, with Clayton just talking to her and working with her with cue cards and picture cards, that child could say a handful of words," Flake told the Associated Press. "When the parents of those types of kids would come in and see the progress that they were making, they would just be in tears and hugging him so much because of his dedication to those kids." He added, "From what I've seen, his attitude is any way he can help children will make him that much happier."

"I enjoy singing and I love performing. There's definitely a thrill you get from performing on stage when everybody's cheering for you, and then there's a completely different kind of thrill when you're working with children," Aiken explained in an interview with Tom Foreman. "You don't necessarily get the applause, and you don't necessarily get the cheers and the pats on the back and everything, but there's a different kind of acceptance. There's a totally different type of feeling of worth when you work with kids."

Aiken says he probably gets along so well with kids because part of him still clings to a childlike innocence, hopefulness, and optimism. "It's just the way I think. It's just the way I act," he said. "I relate to them better because I probably think more like a kid than I do like an adult. I probably act more like a kid than I do an adult."

One of Clay's most appealing attributes to both the kids he worked with and his coworkers has been his sense of humor. "Clay can make me pee in my pants on a regular basis," said Meredith Cox, who also worked with him at the YMCA and is quoted in the *Collegiate Standard*. "He is seriously one of the funniest guys I know. These days, he really gets stereotyped as being this sweet Southern Baptist boy. . . . He is all that, but he also is this really funny guy. He can just be really witty and sarcastic."

It was at Brentwood Elementary School that Clay's natural affinity for kids blossomed into more than just a valued part-time job. Principal Linda McMasters offered Clay the opportunity to manage the school's before-school program. He was still working there when he enrolled in Campbell University, about thirty miles south of Raleigh in Buies Creek. Founded in 1887, the university is the second largest Baptist university in the world. According to its mandate, it promotes both "academic excellence and Christian commitment."

Aiken took evening classes at Campbell because his work at Brentwood had so impressed McMasters that she subsequently hired Clay as a teacher's assistant. He was assigned to Tina Trent's autism classroom, and almost immediately he felt he had found his calling. He decided he wanted a career working with children who had developmental disabilities. To pursue that goal, Aiken transferred from Campbell to the University of North Carolina at Charlotte.

"Working with Tina really made me decide, I'm going to school for this. This is what I want. I want to be as good as she is," Clay said in the *EP Magazine* interview.

During his time at UNCC, Aiken continued working with Trent as a long-term substitute special education teacher. Trent has been enthusiastic about Aiken's ability as a teacher. "Clay was awesome. Autistic students can be very challenging to work with, but Clay welcomed the challenge. He seemed to want to figure them out and make their lives better in any way he could."

Because Charlotte is a three-hour drive from Raleigh, Clay would live at school instead of at home. He was about to embark on a new chapter of his life, filled with new experiences and new friends. As far as he was concerned, he knew exactly where his life was going.

"I fell in love with working with individuals with autism and I planned my life out," Aiken told columnist Fred Bronson. "I was going to teach for six years and then I wanted to go to William and Mary to get my master's in administration. At the same time I wanted to become a principal—that's how I saw myself at fifty years old."

That didn't mean that Clay was planning to turn his back on music. While teaching was his vocation, music remained his personal passion. For his high school graduation gift, Faye had surprised him with recording studio time so that he could make CDs of some of the songs she most enjoyed hearing him sing, including "Dream Lover," "Unchained Melody," and "Don't Let the Sun Go Down On Me." Clay also continued to perform in festivals, showcases, and variety shows, where he would offer the CDs for sale—but it never occurred to him to send the CDs to record companies. "No. I was totally content with my life and thought this would be a good hobby," he said in a *Chart Beat* interview.

Clay settled into an enjoyable routine at UNCC. By day he would take classes, and at night and on weekends he would pursue his musical "hobby." In addition to performing and singing at weddings, Aiken also hosted and co-produced a local variety show, the North Carolina Music Connection, held at Johnston Community College. Surprisingly, although his close friends knew Clay sang at weddings, nobody really suspected just how talented he was, and most of his teachers were completely unaware of his musical skills. Instead, they just knew him as a dedicated, if occasionally eccentric, student.

One of Clay's professors, Fred Spooner, described him in *Clay Aiken Unplugged*, the *Collegiate Standard*'s Farewell Commemorative to Clay, as intelligent and "a little goofy, but I mean who at twenty-two or twenty-three is not goofy. There are some pillars in the classrooms, and Clay would not sit in the chair, he would sit on top of the seat, and put his feet in the chair and lean up against one of the pillars in the back of the room. All the time being very responsive, very cooperative." Spooner said Clay's unorthodox choice of seating didn't bother him, "but I think that bothered some people. But in terms of being quirky and goofy, I think that just added to it."

Clay's closest friend in college and roommate his senior year, Amy Pusey, said Clay is one of the most outgoing people she's ever encountered. The two met in a group at a special ed meeting. Pusey recalled in *Clay Aiken Unplugged* that a professor there said, "'Look around, these are the people you are really going to get to know because you are going to see them a lot.' Clay was kind of the first one to stand up. You could tell that he had a funny personality. He was just so outgoing and wanted to be the person to break the ice."

Pusey remembered how his directness could take people by surprise. "In class one time, he had these sandals and . . . no matter what you do these shoes start to get to where they smell really bad." She and another of Clay's good friends, Angela Coachman, gently tried to tell Clay it was time to buy new shoes because others were beginning to notice. "A couple of days earlier another classmate had already said something. 'It's Clay's feet. It really stinks!'"

Instead of being embarrassed, Clay turned the situation into a performance. Amy reported Aiken stood up and said: "Okay! Excuse me everybody! Somebody is complaining about my feet!" So he took his shoes off and good-naturedly put the offending peds out in the hall.

Pusey loves how quick-witted Clay is. "He is one of those people who can think of a comeback real quick. He is pretty quick in making fun of himself too. He is just that comfortable that it does not bother him. He will make fun of me but not in the way that I will take seriously, where he would say something mean to me. I think Clay would only make fun of the people who would know it was a joke and only with people he's comfortable with and who are comfortable with him. He does it to people who can take it and can dish it out back at him."

Nancy Cooke, who was Clay's professor for the class "An Introduction to Mental Retardation," agreed that Clay has a lightning quick wit. "[He is] very articulate and he has charisma," she observed in UNCC's farewell commemorative to Aiken. "Those are characteristics that help someone to be a good leader or a teacher like he is. Those are all characteristics of his that also helped contribute to his success here at UNC Charlotte."

With his slender frame and glasses, Clay was a stereotypical geek. The fact that he always brought his laptop to class reinforced that image. But what his classmates and professors didn't know was that half the time Aiken wasn't really taking notes—he was actually playing computer games.

That doesn't mean Clay wasn't dedicated. According to Amy, Clay never had to spend a lot of time cracking the books because he was able to intuit what was needed. And as his studies progressed, Clay became ever more involved with all aspects of his education. Cheryl Young admits she was a bit taken aback when she interviewed for her teaching position at the university. "Anytime a potential faculty person is on a campus they open it up to interviews and doctoral students will be there," she explained in *Clay Aiken Unplugged*. "Well, Clay was there for my interview. So you think, 'How many undergraduates actually attend a faculty interview and interview potential faculty?' I thought, *I have to watch this kid*. I knew that Clay was going to be, quote, 'different.'"

Young found Clay not only articulate, but also dedicated, passionate about kids, and perhaps just a little skeptical about authority. "I don't want to say he questions authority, but he questions life. He absolutely believes in equity and justice. He's not passive in any way. I believe he doesn't compromise on his values in terms of equity. I think that's what stands out for me."

Aiken seemed to have boundless energy, Young recalled. "Clay was a doer. He jumped into things, to get things done, and he absolutely was passionate about students with disabilities and equity. And he fights for that. I think he does that with everything he does and believes in. Because Clay is so articulate and he's a thinker, he challenges the world. And so he's outspoken." Young says Aiken did his best to be tactful but didn't always succeed. "When you say things that someone doesn't want to hear, if you're challenging their values, then you can't word it in a way that's going to be tactful."

Although Clay would go to Raleigh periodically on weekends to visit his mom, his home was in Charlotte in the apartment he shared with Amy. Pusey and Aiken were more than best friends; they were like family. "He was really easy to hang out with; easy to know and talk to," Amy reminisced in *Clay Aiken Unplugged*. "Clay got me to open up a little bit more because he is so easy to talk to. He also got me to pay attention to the news more, and politics more. But he is not the type of person who pushes his views on you.

"We got pretty close because we are both more like homebodies. Clay is into movies and we like to hang out and watch movies. Some roommates like to go out or stay in their rooms. Clay and I kind of controlled the living room with the TV.

"We used to sing in the apartment, too. I have a karaoke machine and we used to hook it up to the television. We'd sing stuff like from *Beauty and the Beast, From This Moment On* from Shania Twain. . . . I remember during the Winter Olympics, when Charlotte Church and Josh Groban sang the song 'The Prayer,' we started singing that together. That was one of Clay's favorites. He likes Josh Groban. I sang with Clay quite a few times, and wow he was really good! But . . . at the time, I didn't comprehend how good he was."

For food, they would sometimes go to Pizzeria Uno, where Angela worked, but their favorite was an Italian restaurant named Ciros. Usually, they would just get strombolis for takeout. "It's the best stromboli I've ever eaten in my life," Aiken has said more than once.

Not having to worry about his weight, Clay used to treat himself to decadent desserts like banana fudge ice cream and Oreos and anything else slathered in chocolate. Then he began suffering from mysterious chest pains. He discovered the attacks were an allergic reaction to chocolate. He had to adjust his diet—he's also allergic to tree nuts, mushrooms, shellfish, coffee, and mint.

Around that time, Aiken began tinkering with his look. Pusey said when she first met Clay, he had permed his hair, but he straightened it after Amy encouraged him to do so. She also helped him dye his hair darker than his natural red. "Clay was trying to change his look a bit just to get a little more stylish, especially because he was in a class of girls and we were giving him advice about certain things. We always told him we wanted to see how he looked with contacts. I remember him asking me about how he needed to put them in, what he should do. He used to leave class a lot and fix them."

Amy admits she tended to be a bit protective of Clay. "I felt like the mother hen a little bit," she revealed in *Clay Aiken Unplugged*. "Clay is kind of a mama's boy. He is used to getting taken care of by women. I always made sure he would do what he needed to do."

Even though most of the fifteen students in his special ed program were girls, Clay didn't have a girlfriend. High school chum Alisha Puckett confirms Clay wasn't a ladies' man. "He remained low on girls' radar screens until college, when I last saw a few ladies swooning over him," the *Herald-Sun* reported. "I'm still convinced it was his sweet voice that won them over."

Pusey laughs that it certainly wouldn't be his housecleaning skills, telling the *Collegiate Standard*, "He only cleans when it's necessary. He would let dishes stack up at the sink. He would wash one dish when he needed it and when he was done, he would put it back in the sink again. Laundry was not really his thing either." That's why, she concludes, "he needs someone more organized to complement him." She also believes there are other specific qualities Clay would require for any serious relationship.

According to Pusey, she would have to be "a Christian person, first, for sure; a girl who is funny . . . and who would laugh at his jokes but can also give it back to him. Someone who has a good sense of humor and the kind of person who wants to have a good time without being the person who has to go out and drink, and I can't see him with a smoker. Clay is more of a homebody—we never went to clubs—so I think that someone who might want to hang out with him at the house and possibly somebody who is a little neater than he is."

But the way Clay tells it, he was too busy to think about dating. "I had girlfriends in high school," he told *Teen People.* "After that, my social life consisted of work. I taught in an elementary school where a bunch of older ladies worked, so there wasn't much dating material there." In addition to his studies and student teaching, Aiken was elected president of the UNCC Student Council of Exceptional Children in January 2002.

Although Aiken thrived at college, there were some dark times, too. In an interview with Diane Sawyer on *Primetime Live,* Aiken somberly discussed the day his mother called him with news of a family tragedy. "My mom said, 'Your sister Deb, she shot herself last night.' It hit really, really hard."

Deborah Pearce was Clay's half sister—they had the same birth father, Virgil Grissom. By this time Clay's relationship with Grissom had completely deteriorated. So much so that when he was twenty, Clay legally changed his last name to Aiken, his mother's maiden name. But hearing the news of Deborah's suicide left Clay shaken—and feeling guilty. He admitted to Sawyer that Deborah had called him, but he hadn't returned the call because he assumed she was calling to give him grief about having changed his name. Shortly after the call, his mother broke the news of her suicide. *Primetime Live* tried contacting Grissom for a comment, but Vernon had nothing to say, other than, "This is between me and Clay."

In 2002, Clay had to deal with an even closer loss. Ray Parker, suffering from a lung disease, was dying. In an article written for the *Virginian-Pilot,* Clay's cousin, Karen Santos, remembered one of the last times she saw Clay while he was in college. "It was at the hospital in my uncle Ray's room. Clay and I talked about his studies in special education, his love for children and his work with autistic children." Ray Parker died on the Fourth of July in 2002. Santos said, "A few weeks later I got a chance to hear Clay sing again. Only this time it was at my uncle Ray's funeral."

After the passing of his father, Clay seemed to devote himself even more to achieving his goal of becoming a teacher. He was inspired in great part by a young boy who would change Aiken's life.

Chapter Five
The Best-Laid Plans

Clay once told a reporter, "I would love to be known as a generous and selfless person." To the parents of the children he worked with, Aiken was that and much more.

"There is something about Clayton—he just walks into a room and fills up the room," Mimi Shinn, whose autistic son, Nicolas, was cared for by Clay, told UNCC's campus newspaper.

Although Clay was drawn to autistic children, there is a wide range of clinically recognized developmental disabilities, from Down syndrome to cerebral palsy to learning disorders. The determining factor is whether the person afflicted "has some adaptive challenges—cognitive and/or physical disabilities—and has difficulty managing his or her tasks of daily living," Wendy Wood explained to *Spotlight Health.* Wood, an associate professor of special education at UNCC, stressed that being developmentally disabled doesn't equate with retardation. "Individuals with intellectual disabilities are typically identified by IQ measures," said Wood. "But a person with cerebral palsy might have a normal or even above-average IQ yet still may have issues related to performing tasks of daily living. This person would still be considered developmentally disabled."

According to the nonprofit organization Best Buddies International, the number of people with developmental disabilities in the United States has been estimated as high as 10 million. As it happens, North Carolina runs one of the most progressive programs in the country for teaching children with developmental disabilities. The program is known as CAP-MR/DD—Community Alternatives Program for Persons with Mental Retardation/Developmental Disabilities. It was through this state agency that Clay began working with children whose disabilities were more severe.

"I fell in love with working with the kids," Aiken revealed in an interview with John Morgan. "Kids with autism and developmental disabilities think differently—their view of the world is much more pure and innocent."

While working with an agency in Charlotte called Autism Services, Clay was assigned to the Bubel family, whose fourteen-year-old son Mike had been diagnosed as autistic when he was two. "They are such an inspiration to me. I bonded very closely with . . . Mike and the whole family. I liked that they didn't make excuses for Mike. They didn't expect him to get special treatment but simply to be included like a normal citizen."

Mike's mother, Diane, was aware of how demanding it could be working with her son. It requires "patience and true respect for these children as people first. Mike's autism is severe so one of his biggest challenges is communication," Bubel explained in *Spotlight Health*. "He cannot speak, and he can't always process what is said to him. You can't just tell him things like 'Put your shoes on,' so it can be very difficult. But once you have a child with a disability you have a choice: You can suffer with it or you can choose the happy road. We chose the latter."

They also chose Aiken. "Clayton walked in the door with unconditional love and no expectations," Diane recalled. She added, "It's rare to find people that open and understanding."

Bubel says whenever a new worker would be assigned, she would have to train them to make sure they could handle her son, but she said for the first time she didn't have to do that with Clay. "It was a wonderful match," she said in an interview with Maryann B. Hunsberger. "Clayton respected Mike and tried his hardest to understand him. He realized that Mike's actions weren't just to be dismissed as some behavior, but there was a reason why Mike would do the things he did, and it was our job to try to help him by figuring it out.

I loved that about Clayton. He went beyond what he had to do. He almost became like one of the family."

Bubel remembers Clay showing almost saintly calm. "There were moments, and I like to call them 'autism moments,' when Mike would have a meltdown in public like he was a two-year-old toddler," she said in a *Herald-Sun* profile. "When he melts down in public it's really kind of an ugly scene. Clay was never at all bothered, worried, embarrassed, nothing. Sometimes he'd actually tell the people: 'You need to go about your business. You should understand that there's something different about this child and it's not helping that you're standing there, staring at us.'"

When Clay was assigned to Mike, the boy was at a particularly fragile time. Because of a recent medication change, he would frequently fly into violent rages. Diane recounted to *EP Magazine:* "Mike would punch the heck out of him Monday and Clay would come back Wednesday as if there was nothing wrong and that was just the way you work. He kept coming back. Who does that?

"It was almost a big brother and little brother scenario. Clayton was very comfortable with Mike. I don't really think Mike could do anything that would upset or anger him."

Despite the meltdowns and setbacks, Clay was able to make heartening progress with Mike. In addition to taking Mike out into the local community so that he could learn to handle interactions with strangers, Aiken also taught him basic daily living skills that would help him be that much more independent and self-sufficient as he grew older. He spent hours and hours just playing with Mike. Their favorite things to do included jumping on the family trampoline or just playing tag in the yard.

Working with Mike Bubel gave Clay a new perspective. "What I learned from the Bubels was a no-excuses take on having a child with a disability," he explained in an *EP Magazine* interview. "The whole family knows that there are things that Mike will not be able to do that other children can do, and there are things that he will be able to do that other children can't do. But, that's just a part of life. They don't make any bones about it. It's just . . . 'He is a child, a part of our family, a part of society and that's all you need to know about him.' That really moved me and made me think, *You know what? They're exactly right*."

Aiken feels it's the Bubels who should get all the credit, not just for how they have accepted their son, but for the way they opened their hearts and home to Clay. "They not only welcomed me into their lives, but entrusted me to help care for their most precious gift—their son. He continues to be my inspiration and motivation to help children with disabilities." Because of his experiences specifically with Mike, Clay told journalist Chet Cooper, "Working with individuals with autism is what I planned to do with my life."

But Diane—and Mike—Bubel would play a big part in delaying that particular dream by convincing Clay to pursue a dream of another kind. She can't remember exactly when she first heard Clay sing, but Diane remembers how it came about. "He carried a laptop around and one day clicked on some songs he recorded." She was so surprised to learn of Clay's talent, she insisted he sing a song for her and Mike on the spot. "Then he sang for us live and we were shocked that he had this amazing voice." Right then and there, Bubel suggested that Clay try out for *American Idol,* which would be holding auditions at the Fox affiliate in Charlotte, WCCB.

Thinking that was "the funniest thing" he ever heard, Aiken recalled to Maryann B. Hunsberger that he rolled his eyes and thought, "Yeah, right, like I'm a Justin Timberlake type. They will not take me seriously."

The truth was, Clay did have a secret wish to appear on a television show, but it wasn't *American Idol.* He was an avid *Amazing Race* fan. "It's such a good show," he still enthuses.

Another reason for Clay's lack of enthusiasm for *American Idol* was that he really wasn't a fan of the show. He had never had the opportunity to watch it, because during its first season most of his time was spent between working with Mike during the school year, and then just being with his father before he passed away.

What he did know about *American Idol*, he didn't like much. "I remember seeing someone sing 'My Girl' and I changed the channel," he admitted in *Billboard*. "I guess you've got to hear Simon speak before you get hooked. You're thinking, *He's so mean! What is he going to say to the next one?* When I got back home I watched the episode where Tamyra [Gray] got kicked off, and I thought, *What a crappy show! She was so good!*" So when Diane told him he had to audition, Clay declined, saying, "No, I want to be on *The Amazing Race*."

"I was addicted to it. I had the application ready to send in and my roommate Amy was going to go with me. I was going to send it in with another person, just in case that team didn't work." But Bubel was adamant. "She kept bugging me." Finally, Aiken caved. "I said, 'Fine. I'll do it if you stop nagging me!'"

The gargantuan task of auditioning tens of thousands of people for the second season of *American Idol* would begin at dozens of small cities around the country, such as Charlotte. Those chosen from these first-round auditions would win a trip for two, including airfare and hotel, to audition at the next level, which kicked off in Detroit, then went to New York, Atlanta, Nashville, Miami, and Austin before winding up in Los Angeles. (Meals and ground transportation would be the responsibility of the contestant.) Most important, rather than waiting in line with no promise of performing, the preliminary winners would be guaranteed an audition at a scheduled time at the next city in front of *American Idol* producers, where other hopefuls would also be auditioning off the street. However, the rules made it clear that even if you didn't win the Charlotte audition, you were free to audition again in one of the other cities.

On October 13, 2002, Clay set off in his Honda for the Fox Charlotte studios, listening to Josh Groban on his CD player. When he got there, he joined three hundred other people, some huddled under blankets, waiting under misting skies to get into the studio. Once ushered inside, Clay and the others had to produce two pieces of identification and were required to turn in a copy of the official rules, along with a talent release form and a signed eligibility statement. In the latter, the contestant stated he or she was a legal U.S. citizen, sixteen to twenty-six years old on the date of the audition, eligible to work in the United States, and a resident of the twenty-two-county Charlotte, North Carolina, television market as defined by Nielsen Media Research. In addition, the participants had to confirm they were true amateurs.

All individuals under contract (for management or for any other type of representation) on the date of their audition for anything entertainment related, even non-musical forms of entertainment (for example, modeling or acting), are NOT eligible to participate in the "Charlotte Idol" or "American Idol" auditions.

The talent release form gave Fox the right to use footage from the audition for broadcast, which is why participants were strictly forbidden from wearing clothes with any kind of logo or that had the likeness of any celebrity, dead or alive. Logos weren't allowed because producers wouldn't want the show's advertisers to get upset seeing a competitor's logo in the show; and celebrity images are copyrighted, so if someone were wearing an Elvis T-shirt, for example, Fox could very well have to pay a licensing fee if they wanted to broadcast the audition of the person who wore the shirt. Anyone who forgot or disregarded this rule would be required to turn his shirt inside out.

In an effort to make sure the audition process was fair, anyone found guilty of cutting in line would be immediately disqualified. Plus, it wasn't allowed to hold a place in line for someone for more than a few minutes.

People had started arriving for the audition on the day before, including some hopefuls from West Virginia. When studio officials opened the gates at 8:00 A.M. Sunday, the line was already the length of a football field. After the paperwork was finished, the contestants were instructed on how the auditions would be conducted. They would perform in front of four local judges, who would select the winner, according to the official rules, "at their sole discretion based on vocal ability, performance, style and personality." The participants were asked to tell the judges their name, age, hometown, and what song they were going to sing. They were required to perform a cappella, which means with no musical accompaniment, for no longer than a minute.

Inside the studio, people milled about, waiting for their turn, as only small groups were taken in before the judges. Some people sat quietly while others practiced their songs; singing could be heard in the hallways and coming from the bathrooms. Occasionally, singing could be heard coming from the auditorium, along with applause from the contestants in the audience. Over the course of the day, the judges listened to everything from country to pop to even "The Star-Spangled Banner."

The contestants were graded in four categories, from 1 to 10. The four judges were Scott Bauer, director of Central Piedmont Community College's arts and communication school; Lonnie MacFadden, music director for Swing 1000; Ramona Holloway of 107.9 The Link; and freelance television producer Anne Oberlander, who manned the stopwatch.

Not everyone was allowed to finish the song. Sometimes, Oberlander would interrupt the performance with a curt "Thank you," and the next contestant would be called up. Finally, it was Clay's turn. He introduced himself and told the judges he would sing "Somewhere Over the Rainbow." Typically, his soulful voice would fill the auditorium, but the judges couldn't get past his nerdy appearance, with his unkempt red hair, freckles, and glasses.

Later Ramona Holloway would somewhat defensively tell Leigh Dyer of the *Charlotte Observer* that while Clay had the voice, he didn't have the look of a pop star. "It was just like Opie being the next American Idol," she said. "At the time it didn't appear that Clay had the whole package."

Instead, the judges decided that Quiana Parler, a twenty-three-year-old from Charleston who sang "I Will Always Love You," was the best the Charlotte audition had to offer. They announced she had been named the Charlotte Idol.

Amy Pusey remembers that Clay's response to hearing the winner was a simple "Oh, well." Pusey told the *Collegiate Standard* that Clay "had actually complimented her a lot and said that she was really good. And that he wasn't really surprised. It didn't affect him that much and I don't think it discouraged him at all."

Looking back now, Amy thinks that Clay had already decided to try again. "I think he was used to being in front of crowds but it was kind of like a test run to see how he'd be in an actual audition like that. He knew that the Charlotte audition wasn't the big one; that was just going to be his chance to get to be in Atlanta."

Both Amy and Diane Bubel encouraged Clay to make the trip to Atlanta and try again. But, Amy admits, "I didn't really know what was going to come of it. I knew he was really good but . . . I did worry about his looks and so did he."

After experiencing the Charlotte audition, Clay was determined to give himself another chance, just to see what might happen. His attitude was, if he made it to the next level, it would be a great adventure, and if he didn't, he would come back, finish his degree, and begin his life of teaching children with disabilities, content with the knowledge he had at least given himself the opportunity to fulfill a fantasy.

Aiken couldn't know that his wildest dreams were about to come true.

Chapter Six

Georgia on My Mind

Once Clay had made the decision to trek to Atlanta, there was no reason to keep his passion for singing a secret. Plus, he needed to explain to his professors why he'd be missing class for a couple of days.

According to *Clay Aiken Unplugged,* Priscilla Brame, who was one of Clay's favorite professors, was shocked to hear her student was going to audition for *American Idol.* "He came into my office and he told me that he was going to do *American Idol* and I said, 'Clay, can you sing?' And he said, 'Yeah, I can sing.' His friend, Amy, was with him and I said, 'Amy, can Clay sing?' And she said, 'Yeah, he can sing.' I knew he was singing for weddings, but I had no idea his talent is such that it is."

Seeing Professor Brame's surprise, Clay e-mailed her an audio file of him singing "Open Arms." Brame was so touched, she cried. "I was caught off guard because I was not prepared for such a rich soulful voice that touches the heart and stirs the soul."

At least Professor Brame knew what *American Idol* was. Fred Spooner admitted to the *Collegiate Standard,* "I had no idea what the show was. I said, 'What the hell are you doing? Why are you wasting your time and your money doing this when your profession is going to be special ed?'" Spooner would go on to say that even if Clay made it to Hollywood, he worried about how he could make a living.

Cheryl Young was equally skeptical. "When Clay came and told me that he was going to Atlanta to try out for *American Idol,* I thought, *Yeah, everybody wants to be a rock star,*" she said in *Clay Aiken Unplugged.* "I had no idea he sang, so I said to him, 'Well, okay, go ahead. As long as you make up the work. Good luck. Just make sure you do your work.'"

While Aiken might claim he's not a competitive person, he certainly isn't oblivious. Realizing that his biggest drawback to advancing past Atlanta was his appearance, Clay went shopping for some new clothes. For most of the previous year, Clay's "uniform" had been khakis, T-shirts, and flip-flops. Amy and Angela suggested he try a more preppie look, with button-down shirts and jeans, and shoes that didn't show his feet.

Armed with his new outfits, Clay drove to Atlanta early and camped out until officials showed up to hand out the coveted wristbands. Compared to Charlotte, the Atlanta audition was a human zoo, with 6,500 participants. As Fox had made clear, just showing up was no guarantee you would necessarily get to audition. Producers also reserved the right to pick people out of the line at random, so it wasn't always a case of first come, first served. But Clay managed to get the wristband that signified he was one of those selected to sing.

Clay found himself inside a human assembly line, with assistants barking orders in an effort to keep the lines moving. The participants handed in their paperwork and then were led to the room where they would wait to be called for their audition. This time, if he made it past the first two rounds, Clay would not be performing in front of local judges, but in front of Simon Cowell, the acerbic *American Idol* judge who was also a highly successful record producer, and Randy Jackson. (Singer Paula Abdul did not fly to Atlanta, begging off because she had a previous engagement.)

For the second season, producers had made a few changes in the series. They added a fourth judge, New York hip-hop performer and radio personality Angie Martinez. It was also decided to have Ryan Seacrest serve as sole host, and let Brian Dunkelman go. When asked about Brian's departure, Seacrest claimed, "Dunkelman's doing standup somewhere. He's pursuing his comedic acting, and wants to be on a sitcom, so he won't be with us this time."

Co-executive producer Ken Warwick added, "It was always clear, from a production point of view, that, sort of, Ryan was the leader of the pair, and in truth, there was never enough time in the show to do everything we wanted to do, to get all the kids' profiles, reactions. So when [Brian] said he had other areas he wanted to pursue, it was an obvious thing to say, 'Go and do them freely.'" However, Brian would later express resentment at having been dumped in favor of Seacrest.

In Atlanta, the only thing on the minds of the would-be Idols was getting the chance to audition. Some waited nervously; others exuded confidence, such as South Carolina hopeful Josh Strickland, who was profiled in the *State,* a South Carolina newspaper, by Jaymi Freiden.

Described as "boy-band handsome," Josh, wearing wristband number 5003, was the winner of the Greenville tryout. He had no problem visualizing himself on a plane to Hollywood, following in the footsteps of Kelly Clarkson. A vocal performance major at the College of Charleston, Strickland was bubbling with enthusiasm. "I'm thankful every day that I have this voice. Why should I keep it inside? I'm so ready."

And he was so happy he wasn't one of the thousands waiting outside without a scheduled appointment. But the cattle call atmosphere and the boundless optimism of the people who flocked to the audition just added to the excitement. The fascinating thing for *American Idol*'s supervising producer, David Goffin, was how many people truly believed they had the talent to win.

"People don't understand odds or ratios," he observed to Freiden, "and that's why you get the tears."

And sometimes, the anger. It was reported that one girl, who was summarily dismissed in Atlanta, warned Seacrest on her way past that the judges would be sorry for dissing her. A short time later, she was apprehended trying to sneak back inside, and security discovered a spork tucked in her waistband.

Simon Cowell said he's amazed at the self-delusion he sees. Even the least talented people "all believe that they can sing. There was a guy in Atlanta," he recalled, referring to Keith Beukelaer, "who I thought was the worst singer in the world. Because I cannot believe anyone on this earth can sing as bad as him. He, honest to God, believed he was going to be the next superstar in America. It was so bad that one of the security guards actually collapsed." Cowell laughs at the memory. "This is a true story. He actually fell down flat. I thought someone had shot him. And he was dragged out of the room, because this guy was unbelievable. Maybe there's a medical term which we don't know about. It's either they're deaf, they're insane—I honestly don't know what it is. I mean, I know I can't sing. I've only got to hear myself to prove the point. And these people come in and they really, really genuinely believe that they're good."

But for Strickland, it was nothing but smiles when the judge announced after his performance, "Congratulations. You are the first one I'm advancing."

Then it was time for Clay to see if he, too, had what it took to be worthy of consideration.

Aiken would later tell *Billboard*'s Fred Bronson that the first round of auditions in Atlanta was the most stressful, "because I didn't want to get cut on Sunday and have to drive back on Monday and have everybody say, 'I thought you were going to be gone for auditions.'

"Patrick Lynn was the producer who picked me, and I was the only person of his who made the top twelve."

Unlike in Charlotte, where Clay had chosen his song in advance, in Atlanta he was undecided what to perform up until the last second. "I thought 'Unchained Melody' was too slow. Right before I went in, I decided I'll do 'Always and Forever.' I stepped forward and what comes out of my mouth, I'm not kidding you—the theme song to *Perfect Strangers,* the TV show. He dismissed everybody else and said, 'Sing something else. That was a little stagy.' No kidding! Then finally I sang 'Always and Forever' and I stuck with that."

That Wednesday, Aiken auditioned for co-executive producer Nigel Lythgoe, who, Clay says, "scared me to death because he said, 'I don't care how good you can sing. I don't care if you're the worst person in the world. I'm looking for someone that I can put on a TV show. I'm looking for someone with personality.' Well, that scared me, because I didn't really have one. So I was very nervous. I sang 'Always and Forever' and he said, 'You're a crooner. I don't know if that's a good thing or a bad thing, but I'll let you through. When you sing tomorrow, I want you to really sing it to Paula.'"

But of course, Paula was the one judge who wouldn't be in Atlanta. Clay took a deep breath and told himself, "I'm just going to go in and have a good time. There's no way I'm going to make it. I might as well enjoy myself."

Prior to singing, producers had tried to prepare the auditioning performers for the criticism they might receive. "We spoke to them beforehand to say forget the fact that you've seen this before on TV. You've just got to give it a good audition; you've got to give it back, even if you don't like what we're going to say to you."

However, the response to Clay was thoughtful. When he finished singing, the two judges seemed unsure what to say, because what they had heard didn't jibe with the person they were looking at. Finally, they told him that while they thought he had a great voice, he needed a makeover. Later Aiken would tell the *Winston-Salem Journal,* "It's a compliment, to me, that they liked the way I sang. I'm not looking for approval from them on how I look, really. . . . If they had told me I looked great but sang horribly, I would have taken that a lot worse."

Clay revealed to Bronson an exchange he had with Cowell that was not included in the television clip. "The only thing that was cut was when Simon said, 'The girl who came in before you looks like a pop star, but she has nowhere near the voice you have. We're looking for a pop star, but you have a great voice. What do we do?' And then I said, 'Put me through and let America decide,' which I'm glad they cut because I would have sounded like an idiot.

"Looking back on it I think, *How many times did I deserve to get cut?* Or *how many times was I right on the line?* That first day, there were seven thousand people in that room. They could have just said, 'We've got too many today. We're going to let him go,' or 'The person who comes in next might be better.' There was a guy in my group of five who was just as good as me, and he didn't make it through. Nigel could have let me go because he didn't think I had enough personality. Simon clearly had reservations, but he let me through anyway."

Clay also explained what led to him answering Simon's question of why he was auditioning by saying, "Because I am the American Idol!" Aiken said that prior to the audition Cowell came out and warned, "If we ask you if you're the American Idol, you better not say, 'I hope so.' You better not say, 'I think so.' You better say, 'Yes.'" Clay continued, "He wanted confidence and so I came in and I said it. I didn't necessarily believe it, but I had to say it because I was afraid that's what I needed to get through."

In the end, the most important thing anyone said was when they told Clay, "You're going to Hollywood!"

Back in Charlotte, Amy was taking a test when her cell phone broke the silence. It was a stunned and excited Clay, bursting with the news that he had made the cut and was one of the 200 contestants the show planned to take to Los Angeles.

Because of the astounding turnout, the producers would end up selecting 234 contestants. This group would be whittled down to 32 finalists, who would compete for the American public to be the next Idol. Where the first season had attracted 10,000 hopefuls, over 50,000 people showed up to audition for *American Idol 2*.

RealityTVRules.com, which followed the second season in minute detail, gave a tongue-in-cheek thumbnail overview of what the judges confronted in their cross-country search:

Miami—*6000 people turn out for this audition.*
They get a shaky Shakira, a look-alike Mariah, Edgar a wanna-be Enrique, and another thing they get is a lot of attitude.

Detroit—*6000 people again.*
It looks like all they have to give us is bad dancers, bad stage acts, and a lot more bad attitudes.

Nashville—*5000 hopeful people turn out*
They didn't find any Faith Hills but they did get an opera diva, an eager beaver, someone lying about their age, and yep, more attitude.

Atlanta—*6500 turn out*
They get some good girls, even some great girls, and some good ole southern attitude, all from Atlanta.

Austin—*6000 more hopeful souls*
Bruce Lee turns up, a munchkin, even Harry Potter, and you guessed it more attitudes.

Los Angeles—*11,000 turn up to try out*
They say this is where the real talent is but all they got was Dorothy from Oz, Tarzan, even the lion king took a shot, and that good old attitude turned up again.

New York—*9000 turn out*
Identical twins sing "Fallen" and they are fabulous, unbelievably in tune with each other. Simon wants to only pick one but they both end up going to Hollywood.

While the judges were prepared to sit through a range of performances, there were also unexpected situations. Internet Movie Database reported that in Austin, Texas, brothers Jimmy and Scott Osterman warbled a painful rendition of Paula Abdul's past hit, "Opposites Attract." Just as Simon Cowell was about to rip their performance apart, the "brothers" took off their disguises and revealed themselves to be British performers Ant McPartlin and Declan Donnelly, who in addition to hosting *Pop Idol,* the UK version of the show, have their own comedy show. They had taped their faux performance to air on their comedy show, *Ant and Dec's Saturday Night Takeaway.*

Some people found it hard to take no for an answer. After Miami's off-key Edgar Nova was dismissed, he cut into the tryout line, telling the other contestants he had earned a callback. He refused to leave and had to be removed by security. Undaunted, he flew himself to Los Angeles, donning a disguise so that nobody would know who he was. Still, he was immediately recognized. Rather than booting him out, the producers allowed him to perform—and he was dumped even quicker the second time.

Overall, though, Randy Jackson thought the talent assembled for *American Idol 2* was overall superior to the first year. "I think kids that didn't believe in the show in the beginning, like a lot of people didn't believe, came out and said, 'You know what? This thing works. It's one of the best ways for me to get noticed and to have it happen for me. I'm going for it.'"

Cowell agreed, but added, "Well, to be honest with you, all that happened because we had 50,000 people turn up is we had 40,000 people who couldn't sing." Simon also said that some people were trying to be intentionally bad just to get a noticeable moment on television. "As far as I know, there were three people who got through the net, no question about it, who were there to get themselves on TV, to say to their friends that they sung badly and were humiliated. We spotted them a mile off. And we dealt with them in exactly the same way. Every time we let them audition, they sang badly on purpose. And we said, 'Actually, you know what? You're really good. You don't realize how good you are. You actually have a talent.' They went—*'Whaa . . . ?'* and off they went."

By the time Clay returned to Charlotte, *American Idol* had announced that its newest judge, Angie Martinez, had quit after attending three auditions. The show would proceed with just Abdul, Cowell, and Jackson. In a statement released to the press by Fox, Martinez explained her decision. "Being asked to join *American Idol* as their newest panelist was an honor. However, after judging the first few auditions, I've decided to leave the show because it became too uncomfortable for me to tell someone else to give up on their dream, especially when I realized that many of them have supported my musical career. I thank everyone at Fox for the opportunity and wish every contestant the best of luck."

Although some in the media speculated Martinez had left because of a personality conflict with Cowell, others involved with the show say it was both a personal and a business decision. Producer Warwick said, "She tried it and in truth, she wasn't comfortable in telling a kid that they were no good." Executive producer Cecile Frot-Coutaz also admitted, "The reality is that she was promoting her own album. She had just had an album that had just been released and it's very hard when a kid walks in and tells you he loves your album, he supports you, and then you turn around and tell him he's just no good." Randy Jackson also observed that if "you get up and tell a kid 'You suck,' I don't think that kid's going to say, 'I'm going to buy your album, I'm going to go out and say she sucks, too.' You've got to have a super thick skin to do that."

While the *American Idol* team was busy preparing for the next phase of the competition, Aiken was back in Charlotte making arrangements with the university to take some time off after the first of the year, which meant putting his student teaching on hold. In the meantime, Clay returned to his classes and tried to resume a normal schedule. But as news of his *American Idol* success became known, people were suddenly interested in his singing, which surprisingly got mixed reactions.

When Clay came back to school, Amy threw a small celebratory party, where one of their classmates asked to hear Clay sing. He performed a Luther Vandross song that seemed to impress everybody. But privately, Amy harbored some unspoken doubts. "We all went, 'Yeah, he's pretty good!'" she said in *Clay Aiken Unplugged*. "But we didn't say, 'Wow! He's going to be the next American Idol.'"

Professor Cooke recalled the time the Student Council for Exceptional Children, of which Clay was president, decided to throw a semiformal get-together at a local church. They invited the different group homes for adults with developmental disabilities they had visited as part of a school assignment. Professor Cooke says she urged Clay to sing for everyone. He eventually relented, but only after Amy agreed to sing a duet with him.

In a commemorative magazine published by UNCC's newspaper staff, Professor Cooke said Clay was still "very humble, almost shy," about his singing. "He gave me a copy of a CD he had done long ago, and said, 'You don't have to listen to it if you don't want to.' He was just so embarrassed."

At the party, Clay and Amy sang Shania Twain's "From This Moment On," and Professor Cooke and the others "all applauded and hooted. It was just great! And the residents were clapping and happy and they were singing too. It was just really fun! I guess you could say I understood why he wanted to compete in *American Idol*."

In January 2003, Clay stepped on the plane that would take him to Los Angeles, where he would come face to face with his destiny, whatever it would prove to be.

Chapter Seven

An *American Idol* Roller Coaster

The second season of *American Idol* was scheduled to begin on January 21, 2003. Of the 234 competitors chosen from the seven regional tryouts, only 32 would be left standing by the end of the second week. Interestingly, Atlanta had accounted for 46 of the 234, the most of any city.

Prior to the first episode, Simon Cowell and the producers participated in a press conference to talk about the upcoming season. There, Simon defended his stage-side manner, saying that telling people the truth is simply being a responsible music producer, especially since many of the lesser-talented hopefuls are often inappropriately encouraged by friends and loved ones. "I think it's called 'suspending your disbelief.' Everyone in the world now wants to be famous, and what they don't understand is you need something called talent. And their friends and their family say they're good. And we're there to say, 'No, you're not.'"

Simon added that despite his image, there had been times when he had held back and not spoken his mind the first season. "As I reached the end of the first series, I sat there and I bit my tongue on the last two or three shows because I thought, *I'm going to work with these people. Maybe I should be nice to them.* I bit my tongue and I wish I hadn't. I will never, ever do that again, because I regret the fact that I behaved that way, because there were certain things I would have liked to have said on those last couple of shows and I didn't. But I will next time."

When pressed to give an example, Cowell said, "Well, one of the things I may have said is I would have told Nikki McKibbin to go back to the strip club. I know it sounds unkind but I believe you should say what's in your mind. And as I watched her, I thought, *You are a better stripper than you are a singer*. And I know that sounds rude but that's what I felt. The point I'm trying to make is, not to be unpleasant for the sake of it but I think when you're judging these shows you have to be honest."

However, Simon had positive things to say about the level of ability among the *American Idol 2* participants who did have the talent to compete, particularly when compared to the first season. "To me it's a very, very different competition. I think what we've seen in six months is a huge sea change between *American Idol* and *American Idol 2*. What I've noticed this time around is there was much, much less stage school this time. What you're going to see in the finalists compared to the first season is literally all shapes and sizes. I mean, this show totally will fail or succeed based on who turns up, the characters. . .—if it was all stage school brats, you wouldn't have a show."

At the same time, Cowell observed a greater level of what he deemed "desperation" on the part of those auditioning, because after seeing Kelly Clarkson go on to become a star, people saw how this competition could change lives. "Let me tell you, every single person who came in and actually stood in front of us was absolutely desperate to get praise and to go through to the next round. They really, really were *there*."

Upping the ante for this crop of competitors was the involvement of famed music executive Clive Davis, who Cowell said was "overseeing all of the musical stuff for us now. If Clive didn't believe in this project he wouldn't have got involved and he's 101 percent committed to making the existing artists, and the new artists, successful recording artists."

With the departure of Angie Martinez, the producers had decided to invite guest celebrity judges to participate in the later shows. And if anyone thought the occasionally hostile interaction between Cowell and Paula Abdul was a show for entertainment purposes, Simon put that notion to rest. "You know, I'm not going to lie. I mean, we don't get on particularly well. But you have to take it a day at a time. With a show like this, I think what you have to try and do before you turn up for each filming section is to disregard what's happened before, do your job, which is you're there to judge talent. And if she irritates me, which she probably will, I'll tell her to shut up. And she'll do the same to me. But it's not something which you should be premeditated [preoccupied] about."

Although the themes for the final ten episodes had not yet been confirmed, executive producer Frot-Coutaz said fans should expect that once again, the song selection would stay away from current hits. "I think there's much more of a tendency to imitate the current artist, whereas, if you give them a song from the sixties or seventies, chances are that they don't know it very well. They will be much more true to who they are and to their personality, than if they sort of mimic Britney Spears or one of *their* idols."

One interesting lesson Simon learned in the first season was that the performance people see on TV is sometimes very different from what the judges experience watching in the theater, which could go a long way in explaining why on occasion the home audience seems to so sharply disagree with the judges.

"When you're sitting in a live theater and everyone's going nuts behind you and they're screaming and shouting, you hear a completely different performance. And you know, there have been one or two times, where you've said someone was good on the night, then you watched it back on TV, and wonder, *What the hell am I saying?*"

Although Clay couldn't know it when he showed up in L.A. to start the next round of competition, it would be the perception and appreciation of his talent by the people watching at home that would carry Clay through. But first, Clay would have to make it past another round of auditions before he could even think about how he would come across to a national audience.

At Simon's suggestion, the number of audition episodes was increased for the second season of *American Idol*, with the first three shows devoted to footage of the aspiring singers who tried out across the country. The footage included Clay's audition in which he wore an untucked striped shirt, glasses, and the contestant number 5230.

In a posting on the Reality TV Talk Web site, one viewer echoed the same audio double take Cowell and Jackson experienced hearing Aiken perform. "Clay Aiken is quite the nerdmeister. . . . He thinks he could have been in the top ten in the first *AI*. He performs 'Always & Forever.' And guess what? This guy can sing. Really. He may not look like much of a star, but then neither does Beck. The two judges agree that he should work on his style, but with his great voice he's on his way to Hollywood."

The fourth episode of the second season showed the footage taken of the 234 regional selections going through the series of auditions that would winnow the crop down to 32. Clay and the others had arrived in Los Angeles in December 2002 for five days of tryouts, held at the Alex Theatre in Glendale, California, about a twenty-minute drive from Hollywood. Everybody said hello to the judges, and then the competition got under way.

In order to cull the large number of contestants, the performers were put in groups of ten, and they each did a quick snippet of a song. From each group some contestants were approved to go on; others were told they'd reached the end of the *Idol* line. Not surprisingly, emotions ran high, and all around Clay people were crying and looking crushed that their dream was over. Clay had told himself he was just going to enjoy the experience because he knew he had a teaching career to go back home to. But with each round, Clay found himself in the group that was told they were continuing on.

The next round of auditions brought a new twist, requiring the contestants to come up with a melody for lyrics given to them by the judges. For Clay, it was like being back in college, when he would just wing a test because he intuitively knew what to do. While many others struggled, Clay passed this audition and was among the eighty hopefuls left still competing at the end of the second day.

The next task was to see how collaborative the contestants were. They were put in small groups and given a choice of three songs and the opportunity to work with a musical director. After they left the theater and were bused back to the hotel, the personalities of the performers started to emerge. Some of the group immediately made plans to continue working on the songs. Others, mostly guys who were feeling itchy after being cooped up in a theater all day and a hotel at night, made plans for a night on the town in Hollywood.

Clay was typically down the middle. He didn't feel the need to rehearse all night and wouldn't have minded seeing the sights. But when he found out the group going out wasn't interested in sightseeing but planned to check out the nightlife and make it a party, Aiken declined.

The next day started stressfully. Three of the group were AWOL after their late night out, so nobody could leave for the theater. Eventually the three showed up and the bus took off, but clearly there was tension in the air. Cowell was visibly annoyed at the obvious lack of preparation among many of the groups, so by the end of the day only forty-eight were left to continue. Once again, Clay avoided the ax and survived to sing again.

Ominously for any of the group that might have been superstitious, the fourth day of auditions fell on Friday the thirteenth. This day's musical exercise was for the performers to do their own staging while singing a cappella. Although

Clay scored with his ability to sing, he was not very comfortable doing much movement or anything that resembled dancing. He kept his movements contained and hoped for the best.

At last, it was time for the judges to make their final decisions. They organized the contestants into three groups of sixteen, and each group went into a different room. Two of the groups would continue on, one would go home. It seemed fitting that Paula was given the unenviable task of telling Group 2 they had been cut. The tears in that room were full of disappointment, while members of the other two groups whooped it up and cried tears of relief and happiness. Clay was almost numb, amazed he was going to compete in front of the American public to be the next Idol.

The thirty-two finalists were as follows:

J.D. Adams

Clay Aiken

Rebecca Bond

Kimberly Caldwell

Sylvia Chibiliti

Corey Clark

Lashundra "Trenyce" Cobbins

Samantha Cohen

Candice Coleman

Equoia Coleman

Frenchie Davis

Chip Days

Julia DeMato

Meosha Denton

Patrick Fortson

Jennifer Fuentes

Louis Gazzara

Joshua Gracin

Charles Grigsby
Ashley Hartman
Kimberly Kelsey
Patrick Lake
Kimberley Locke
Vanessa Olivarez
Bettis Richardson
Jordan Segundo
Hadas Shalev
Nasheka Siddall
Jacob Smalley
Rickey Smith
Ruben Studdard
George Trice

Clay's family was both stunned and delighted that he was going to be competing on national television. His achievement couldn't have come at a better time. For the past year, Aiken's mom and the rest of the family had been dealing with Ray's diagnosis of pulmonary fibrosis and his subsequent death. The news that Clay was one of the thirty-two finalists was a welcome dose of good news for an emotionally drained family. "God closes doors, and he opens other ones," Faye Parker said in a phone interview with Leigh Dyer. Even though Clay was just one semester away from graduating when he found out he'd be one of the final thirty-two, his mom understood his having to see the experience through. "This is a once-in-a-lifetime opportunity," she said proudly. Clay's younger half brother, Brett Parker, agreed. "As long as he gets to do what he wants, I'm happy," he said.

Starting with the February 4 episode, groups of eight contestants would perform, and the two voted to be the best of the group would move on to be included in the final twelve.

There would also be four "wild cards"—each judge would bring back one of the thirty-two who had not made the initial cut, and one would be voted back by the viewers.

Out of the first group, Charles Grigsby and Julia DeMato moved on; Bettis Richardson, J.D. Adams, Kimberly Caldwell, Lashundra Cobbins, Meosha Denton, and Patrick Fortson were sent home.

The next group scheduled was arguably the toughest, because in addition to Clay it included Ruben Studdard and Kimberley Locke, as well as Candice Coleman, Rebecca Bond, Jacob John, Hadas Shalev, and Jennifer Fuentes. For his performance, Clay had decided to sing "Open Arms," originally made famous by Steve Perry of Journey. Even though Simon and Randy had previously advised him to adjust his appearance to better look the part of a pop star, Aiken was resistant.

In an interview with *Ability* magazine, Clay admitted, "I went into it initially saying, 'If I'm going to lose this, I'm going to lose it on my terms. I don't want anybody messing with me. I'm going to dress the way I want to dress.'" He went on to tell Fred Bronson, "I think there's a difference between appearance and image. An image is not how you look. It's what you do. It's what you portray. Your personality, the example you set, and that's huge for me. I don't have a problem with my image if that's the definition of it, because I think that certain people out there who have the best attire, who have nothing but style, have a bad image.

"But I never really considered appearance to be a problem. I've never seen a pop star wear glasses, so I had to get rid of them. I thought that was it. Apparently I was a lot uglier to start with. You grow up in Raleigh, you don't have Dolce & Gabbana everywhere. You don't have Prada and all that stuff. So I was wearing some Express clothes and I had some khaki pants on and I thought I was looking okay."

The day Clay was to perform, the show was rocked by scandal when Fox gave the boot to popular contestant Frenchie

Davis for having posed topless for a Web site that claimed to offer kiddie porn. Davis claimed she had divulged this information to Fox executives when she came to Hollywood, explaining she had needed the money for college. The network later determined that the incident merited disqualification. Not for legal reasons—since she was eighteen when she took the job, the photos are not illegal—but more over ethical concerns.

Frenchie fans and supporters were shocked, then outraged. An online petition to reinstate Frenchie was started, and many pointed out that in the first season one of the contestants had been a stripper. But as one executive told *E! Online,* "There's an enormous difference between working as a topless dancer and a stripper and someone who's posing on a Web site geared to men's fantasies toward underage girls." The decision was final.

It was a stunning turn of events for the ebullient singer from Washington, D.C., who had called *American Idol* her proudest achievement and who *Entertainment Weekly* had picked as the favorite to win it all. Even Simon Cowell seemed dismayed; he issued a statement saying that his production company would work with Frenchie to help her establish a musical career.

It was the second time an *American Idol 2* contestant had been dismissed. On January 30, Jaered Andrews was abruptly replaced, although the network refused to say why. Early reports suggested that Andrews was let go after a background check turned up he had previously been a member of an Ohio-based hip-hop group called Ordinary Peoples. But the Smoking Gun Web site revealed the real reason Fox dropped him, along with his mug shot "taken after his arrest by Youngstown, Ohio Police in November of 2003, after a bar fight turned deadly." The site goes on to reveal, "According to police, Andrews and some friends were in the Blue Ribbon Grille last November 16 celebrating his selection as an *American Idol* semi-finalist when they began arguing with Thomas Blakeley. Andrews told police . . . that he punched Blakeley once in the face, causing the man to fall back and strike his head on the pavement outside the club. While prone, Blakeley was allegedly struck twice by Jerrold Allen, an Andrews crony who has been charged with aggravated assault. An autopsy found that Blakeley died of blunt force trauma to the head as a result of his skull hitting the pavement." As it turned out, a jury would acquit Andrews on all charges. Even though his *American Idol* chance at fame had slipped away, he still would have his freedom and the possibility of starting over.

Through all the distraction and upheaval, the remaining contestants had to somehow focus on performing and move ahead. Singing "Open Arms," Clay seemed to nail the performance and got high marks from the judges. Paula Abdul called his voice "brilliant" and "magnificent" and told Aiken there was a "great whole vibe about you." Jackson, still unable to equate Clay's appearance with his voice, asked, "Where does that voice come from? . . . Very nice." Even Simon had to admit, "You sang very well," but still doubted that Clay had the whole star package. "When I look at you, I don't think, *There is the American Idol,* but maybe the public will."

But not that evening. Although Clay performed well on the February 11 broadcast, Ruben and Kimberley were stellar, so it came as little surprise to Clay that they were voted the top two and would get to move on. Far from being devastated, Clay took the news with gracious calm, mostly because he knew he still had a chance of making the group of twelve as a wild card.

The day after missing the cut, Aiken talked to *Journal* reporter Tim Clodfelter and was his usual upbeat self. "If it works for me, I will postpone college as long as I need to, and if not I'm ready to go back and teach," Clay said. Then he added with confidence, "Don't put a nail in my coffin—there's still a chance."

But he would have to wait three weeks before learning which road his destiny would take.

Chapter Eight
A Second Chance and Then Some

Because he had come in third in the voting behind Kimberley Locke and Ruben Studdard, and because his vocal ability was now unquestioned, Clay was selected to be one of the wild card contestants for the March 4 episode. The list, announced on the February 26 show, was comprised of five singers from the four semifinal rounds—Clay, Chip Days, Kimberly Caldwell, Nasheka Siddall, and Lashundra "Trenyce" Cobbins—and four who had participated in the "Going to Hollywood" round—Aliceyn Cooney, Janine Falsone, Olivia Mojica, and Carmen Rasmusen.

In the series' second year, the producers had decided to increase the number of wild card selections to four, over two in the first season. One reason to increase the number of finalists was that it gave the Fox network two more episodes for the May sweeps. But from the show's point of view, having more wild card choices gave producers and judges one final opportunity to put forward the best group of finalists possible, such as in Clay's case when a particular semifinalist group of eight was top-heavy with talent or a performer who had the ability to go all the way had suffered from a poorly chosen song. But once the four wild cards were chosen, the fate of the next *American Idol* would solely be in the hands of the viewing public.

The first thing many people noticed when the performers were introduced was that Clay had undergone a subtle but distinct style adjustment. Aiken admits he had been stubborn about wanting to do things on his own terms, including the style he presented, in the earlier rounds. "And then I lost it on my own terms," he said in an interview with Chet Cooper. "So when I came back for the wild card show I said, 'Okay, do whatever you want to do with my hair. That's fine.' I'm very irreverent with my hair. It's not sacred to me. So I said, 'Do whatever looks good. Just make my ears look small.'

"Somebody asked me, 'Aren't you offended when they say you look nerdy?' I'm not, because I don't put any emphasis or stock in that. I don't care. I don't judge a person by how they look, so it doesn't matter. As long as I don't change in my heart and in my head, then I'm the same person. It's just a different wrapping. It wasn't like *Extreme Makeover* where I got a nose job or anything."

But for the wild card show, Clay still insisted on selecting his own clothing. As it turned out, he could have been wearing sackcloth and still have been the cream of that particular episode's crop.

On Zap2it.com, Daniel Fienberg wrote that most of those getting a second chance didn't deserve it. "It became clear that the American voters were pretty spot-on in the early rounds. With only one exception, the also-rans from previous shows were equally so-so on Tuesday night. It was also obvious that the people who didn't even make the semifinals had been eliminated for a reason. Having never performed on live TV before, the inexperienced candidates seemed nervous and out of place. Regardless of what the judges may have said, nobody slipped through the cracks. . .

"The aforementioned exception is Clay Aiken, who has gone from geeky Woodstock look-alike to smoothed polished performer before our eyes. Aiken's rendition of Elton John's 'Don't Let the Sun Go Down On Me' was Tuesday's obvious standout."

The judges agreed, as a transcript of their critique shows.

Paula: Clay, this is what this competition is about. This is what the wild card is about. Big fan, love your hair, you changed your hair. You've raised the bar, we talk about raising the bar, you've surpassed the bar. You are a star, and you've got this confidence about you that is quiet and subtle, that is not intimidating, and you welcome everybody in. Great job.

Simon: Did you like him?

Paula: You know, what I'm trying to say is, yeah, I liked you.

Randy: Did you really like him?

Paula: I really did.

Simon: C'mon, get off the fence here, Paula, I wasn't sure about that.

Paula: Well, come back to me on that one.

Randy: Clay, man, you looking fly, you got your look together, you went away, worked, did whatever you did, it was really, really good. I gotta give you our props. I gotta stand up for you, man. [Randy and Paula give Clay a standing ovation. Simon, of course, stays firmly rooted in his seat.] Right song for the right guy, you did your thing. You came back, you did your homework, I love that. That is what this is about, we hope people come back and do the work, and I still say, where's that voice coming from? God, dude.

Simon: Clay, wow, wow. I was really impressed! And do you know what's interesting is, I mean that was a fantastic performance, really, really fantastic. It's the fact that I think that you don't look like the conventional pop star, actually in a way, is probably a good thing for you because you are so memorable, and you're still looking better each week as well. It was great, really, really great. Well done.

Earlier in the competition, on the night Clay competed in the group of eight, Cowell had singled out Ruben Studdard, telling him, "You are a star. You set the standard for this competition." But on that night, Clay made it clear that he too was going to be a force to be reckoned with. It was a turning point not only in the competition, but for Aiken personally as well.

It was no surprise when the votes were announced the following night: Clay had far and away surpassed the others in votes. Then the judges got to announce their wild card selections: Paula gave the nod to Trenyce, Randy selected Kimberly Caldwell, and Simon chose the seventeen-year-old from Utah, Carmen Rasmusen. "I don't think she'll win the competition," he said later, "but I think she has a spark that none of the other contestants have."

Since he had made it to the final twelve, and considering the compliments he had gotten from Paula and Randy on his looks, Clay became more open to suggestions regarding his stage appearance. "They just said, 'You need help,'" *Ability* magazine reported. "Once I made it to the top twelve I thought, *Well, I'm going any week now, so I might as well let them do whatever they want.*"

And that meant letting the *American Idol* wardrobe supervisor, Miles Siggins, buy clothes for him. "I was really hesitant with clothes because there were certain things I'm not comfortable with," he told *Billboard*'s *Chart Beat*. "I don't like wearing T-shirts. It took me a little longer to warm up to Miles. I didn't let him do anything on that first top-32 show. I came in dressed how I wanted to dress and then on the wild card show, I let him help me a little bit more and then the rest of the show, I finally gave up. 'Miles, I trust you completely. Go ahead and do what you want to do.'"

Starting with the March 11 show, the contestants would be performing in front of a live theater audience for the first time, which increased the excitement quotient for both the home audience and the finalists. Producer Nigel Lythgoe explained, "There is a wall of sound that comes from the audience, which in truth brings a better performance from the artist."

CLAY AIKEN

The theme for this round would be "An Evening with Motown," a fitting homage to guest celebrity judge Lamont Dozier, who, along with writing partners Brian and Eddie Holland, was largely responsible for Motown's unique sound during its heyday in the 1960s and '70s. The songs of Holland/Dozier/Holland include "Baby Love," "Bernadette," "Where Did Our Love Go," "Heat Wave," and "Reach Out, I'll Be There." They were recorded by the likes of Marvin Gaye, the Supremes, Martha Reeves and the Vandellas, and the Temptations.

Prior to the show, the *Detroit Free Press* caught up with Dozier, who revealed he had been a fan of *American Idol* since it premiered, so he was thrilled to be participating, especially with the current crop. "Anything that has to do with music and new voices, the discovery of that new star on the horizon, I'm always looking for that. These young singers have a lot of talent. And a couple of them have a unique sound, a voice and originality to go beyond the show whether they win it or not," said the Detroit native who now makes L.A. his home. He was particularly impressed with Studdard, Aiken, and Vanessa Olivarez, believing each had career potential if they wanted to work hard enough to pursue it. Describing Clay's rehearsal, Dozier seemed amazed. "His voice filled the room. It blew my mind. . . . He's got the sound. His talent is real."

While Dozier's flattery of Clay might have been deserved, Dozier was equally complimentary to every other performer on the March 11 show, a trend that would become the hallmark of nearly every celebrity judge, much to Simon's growing annoyance with each passing week. Since the guest judges had not been watching the contestants week in and week out like Simon, Paula, and Randy, their input came across as less informed, as reflected in these exchanges critiquing Kimberley Locke and Josh Gracin, respectively:

Dozier: Looked like you were ready for business.

Randy: Good, but not the best we've heard.

Dozier: Came with your heart . . . can't ask for more than that.

Simon: You're a marine, take that silly necklace off . . . you could lose a few pounds . . .

While Paula, Randy, and Lamont Dozier enthused over Clay's performance of "I Can't Help Myself,"—"brilliant" . . . "amazing" . . . "the look of a star"—Simon was more reserved, saying that Clay sounded good, "but if I must be honest, it was Motown the Musical."

It was obvious America thought otherwise. The next morning, *USA Today* published an online poll that indicated Clay was suddenly the favorite to win the competition. However, viewers apparently did agree with Simon's observation of Vanessa Olivarez, who performed "You Keep Me Hanging On." He told the twenty-two-year-old from Atlanta that watching her perform reminded him of Bette Midler: "I see you more as an entertainer than what we're looking for in this competition." And indeed, she became the first of the finalists voted off.

By this time in North Carolina, friends, acquaintances, and strangers were cheering on their hometown boy. Clay's ongoing success and the talent he showed created a sense of pride in those who knew him. The *Charlotte Observer* spoke to Professor Cheryl Young, who recalled, "Clay's creativity and ability to motivate others was evident as a student, and these traits shine through on stage." At the same time, it was still sometimes surreal to see him on television and know he was now nationally famous, because she still remembered him as Clayton with the empty fashion plate.

"I'd look at Clay on stage, and with some of the things they have the singers do, like walk around in a circle doing some kind of dopey dance move, I'd think, *Well this doesn't really seem like Clay.*" She was also surprised that he seemed so unperturbed by Simon's sometimes harsh remarks, "because some of the criticism was just seething and Clay can be so outspoken. But Clay is smart. He knows what it is that you have to do. And that doesn't violate anybody's sense of justice or equality."

It was also interesting that among some Clay fans, there was a feeling that Hollywood's gain might be special needs children's loss. Behavior therapist and mother of two autistic sons, Peggy Keller wrote in a foxesonidol.com column, "There are very few nurturing males in the world of special ed, and they are desperately needed considering that autism affects boys 75 percent more than girls. According to the Centers for Disease Control, it has also risen 900 percent in the last decade. Therein lies the reason why I will not be entirely disappointed if Clay does not win the competition. Let the stock boys and the hairdressers become superstars. The real world that contains kids who need funny, kind, patient educators needs Clay."

On the other hand, she hoped, "Perhaps if he does win *American Idol*—or does very well—his story may inspire others to follow him not as a singer, but as a teacher. Unfortunately, those that live in the world of 'special needs' will still need him and others like him. Autism is a lifelong condition."

As far as Clay's mother was concerned, even if he never returned to teaching, Clay would always find a way to stay involved with special needs kids. She also believed that her son was destined to be one of the final two contestants, explaining to the *Charlotte Observer,* "He just keeps the audience eating out of his hand." Faye also approved of Clay's evolving look. "I think he's so cute. He's appealing to the teen girls—and the old ladies, too," she said.

Gladys Knight turned out to be a fan as well. The theme for the second round of the finals was songs from the movies. Aiken performed "Somewhere Out There" from *An American Tail,* originally recorded by James Ingram and Linda Ronstadt. It brought Knight out of her seat to applaud. "You're a mystery. You have your own look. You're magical, and your voice is so pure. Something exceptional will happen for you."

After a beat, Simon drolly added, "I just love songs about mice." But he also acknowledged after that performance, Clay had become the one to beat. Online chat rooms were appalled that Julia DeMato managed to survive another week, as viewers spared her and voted off Charles Grigsby.

Originally, the next show was supposed to be disco night, but at the last minute it was switched to a country-rock theme in honor of guest judge Olivia Newton-John, who had suggested the theme but was only available that week because she was preparing to leave on tour. The genre proved problematic for many of the performers, who seemed to ignore the theme altogether. Simon felt equally lost and told *E!*, "When the first performance came on I thought, *Well, I might as well leave.* I mean the only thing I could comment on was the hat." Olivia also felt the pressure, but for a different reason. "It's harder than you think to come up with something constructive, coming after two people who already said something."

Clay dealt with the theme by pretending he missed the memo and sang a Bryan White tune, "Someone Else's Star." Even though his singing was typically powerful, his seeming hesitation to move away from his power-ballad comfort zone lost him some overall points, especially in light of Ruben's absolutely rocking version of Lynyrd Skynyrd's "Sweet Home Alabama." Simon summed up Clay's performance by noting, "Sweet, but it sounded identical to last week." Still, it was good enough to bring Clay back again. Unfortunately for Julia DeMato, she had finally run out of lives and was sent packing back to Connecticut.

Even though the finalists were still living a fantasy come true, events in the real world had put everything in perspective that fourth week of March 2003 as America initiated a military conflict with Iraq. With the start of the war, Marine Josh Gracin would have to leave Los Angeles and report to Camp Pendleton within twenty-four hours should his unit be called to active duty. However, the *Los Angeles Times* reported that Gracin had a good chance of not being called at all. "Within each unit is a section that might not be called up, and Joshua belongs to one of those sections," Staff Sergeant Chad McMeen of the Marine Corps television and film liaison office said.

The producers had known going into the series that Gracin's duty would always take precedence over the series. "Joshua has been very upfront with us from the very beginning that he might have to leave us," the *Times* quoted co-executive producer Ken Warwick. "He's in contact with his commander, and he might have to go. He's got a lot to lose." But his spot on the show wasn't one of those things—the producers had already told Gracin that if he were called to duty while still on the show, he'd be reinstated as a finalist on a future season without having to go through the audition process again.

Right on the heels of dealing with Gracin's possible deployment, the Smoking Gun Web site dropped a coin on Trenyce and revealed the crooner had once been busted. Accompanying a typically unflattering mug shot, the site gave readers the rundown. "Meet Lashundra Cobbins...better known as 'Trenyce,' one of the nine remaining *American Idol* finalists. And, in the proud tradition of reality TV, the unemployed singer has a rap sheet. Cobbins was busted in October 1999 on a felony theft charge." The report goes on to explain that after completing a pretrial diversion program, her records were expunged. The site also observed, "According to a Q&A segment on the Fox Television Web site, when Cobbins was asked about the most embarrassing moment of her life, she answered, 'I don't have one that I can think of.'"

Although producers refused to comment on Trenyce's arrest, it was confirmed they had known about her past troubles and did not consider it an issue. While the executives had been prepared for Josh's military situation and questions about Trenyce, the revelation about Corey Clark blindsided them and everyone else.

Once again, the bombshell was dropped by the Smoking Gun, which reported on March 31, "An *American Idol* finalist is facing trial next month on charges he assaulted his teenage sister and battled with cops while resisting arrest. Corey Clark, 22, was arrested last October following a disturbance in his family's Topeka, Kansas home. . . . When police arrived, Clark . . . and his 15-year-old sister Alecia were questioned separately by officers. After about 15 minutes, Clark became confrontational with cops, screaming and yelling at officers. . . . Clark was handcuffed behind his back and placed in a Topeka Police Department cruiser. He was booked into the Shawnee County jail and charged with a variety of misdemeanors, including battery on four law enforcement officers, battery on his sister, and endangering a child."

The fallout was immediate. Clark was dismissed for failing to disclose to producers the charges pending against him. And once again, many of the show's fans wondered how the producers missed this detail during the routine background checks done on every reality show contestant.

Daniel Green, who cofounded the Smoking Gun, says it's not necessarily the producers' fault that these bombshells keep falling on all reality shows. "I think certainly the background checks have not always been thorough. There's also a case of when they do the background checks, they are limited in what they can do. The person on the show might give a list of five or ten people to talk to . . . but when the show is broadcast, suddenly hundreds, if not a thousand people who know somebody on the reality program, suddenly say, 'Hey wait. I know that person. He's the guy who I sued ten years ago. I didn't know he was on a reality TV show.' So we have a great advantage that the networks just don't always have."

Fortunately, producers didn't have to worry about any criminal skeletons falling out of Clay's closet. His biggest drama was confined to what song to pick, especially after Simon's on-the-money observation that his second- and third-round songs had been pretty identical in sound, emotion, and presentation. Since the singers had the freedom to choose what they wanted, the onus was on Clay to better show his range.

At the same time, as he told *Billboard,* he didn't want to be *too* influenced by outside criticism. "I've learned to definitely like to trust my instincts. I don't second-guess myself." While the producers had been willing to give an opinion, there was no strong-arming. "No, no, no," he said. "We got the theme and the only restriction we had within that theme was whether or not the song could be cleared." But on occasion, Lythgoe might let someone know he thought they should reconsider. "The executive producer would say, 'I really think you're making a bad choice,' but then would always add, 'Ultimately, it is your decision.' Because of course, they don't want to pick a song for someone and then later, I get cut and I can blame them for picking it."

Those watching Clay at home couldn't help noticing how with each passing round, Clay was growing into an ever more confident and polished performer. Some, like his old roommate Amy, worried that all the success and attention he was getting would change him and cause him to forget his friends back home. But Clay would soon prove to everyone that no amount of success would change who he was or the values he held dear.

Chapter Nine

One Week at a Time

When Clay found out in December 2002 that he had been chosen as one of the thirty-two semifinalists, it was obvious that his success would put a wrench in his graduation plans. Although he had completed all of the necessary classes, he needed one semester of student teaching in order to meet the requirements to get his degree. Before *American Idol* came roaring into his life, he had planned to do his student teaching in the spring of 2003, but instead requested a leave of absence until he knew exactly what his future held.

Aiken's professors were all supportive of his opportunity, and the *Charlotte Observer* reported that they were trying to come up with an alternative assignment for Clay so that he could complete the requirement and graduate in case he won the competition and was unable to return to North Carolina in the near future. "He's such a nice young man, so genuine—we've been so excited for him," said Wendy Wood, Aiken's faculty adviser. "I don't have any fault with young people following a dream."

In her eyes, she had no problem envisioning Clay as a pop idol. "I love the way he looks—I'm much fonder of students who aren't the status quo hunk or beauty queen," said Wood. "I think people who have a different look are more interesting."

At the beginning of the April 1 broadcast, Ryan Seacrest addressed the dismissal of Corey Clark, explaining that it came about because Clark had not been forthcoming about his situation. In a video, Clark apologized for being afraid to be honest with the producers and for taking up one of the coveted finalist slots, but he assured his fans this setback would not keep him down or prevent him from pursuing his dream, because "this is who I am."

From that awkward beginning, the remaining contestants geared up for the round's disco theme, which included judge Verdine White from Earth, Wind & Fire. It proved another difficult genre for many of the contestants. Clay followed his strategy of avoiding any drastic adjustments and performed Carl Carlton's "Everlasting Love." The judges' responses were equally predictable. Randy called him "brilliant," Paula stated the obvious by noting, "his voice is his voice," and White expressed the same wonder as everyone first hearing Clay, marveling, "He doesn't look like he could sing like that." Only Simon seemed annoyed. Besides not liking the genre, he didn't care for Clay's performance and let him know it. In fact, Cowell seemed pained the entire evening. But the following night brought a surprise; because of Corey's dismissal, nobody would be voted off the show that week.

The following week was special for Clay because Diane Bubel and her daughter Emma were flying out as his guests to attend the show. This time, Lionel Richie was on hand to dole out the platitudes.

As it happened, Clay was scheduled to perform first and sang the old Billy Vera and the Beaters hit, "At This Moment." Surprisingly, Simon gave him a complimentary "Well done," but both Paula and Randy seemed disappointed. Randy observed that Clay had been showing less range the last two weeks, but it was Paula's comment that got to the heart of the matter, as it were—that she couldn't feel any heartbreak in the song. And for good reason: Clay admitted he'd never had his heart broken. "I know it will happen, either romantically or just in general with someone I trust. But I am the type of person who can prepare myself for it." Nor did Clay think he'd ever broken anybody else's heart. "I mean, come on, hello! The way I see it, I'm not that big a prize."

It was ironic that the man who was becoming an American heartthrob had never been in love. He said in a *J-14* Q&A, "I don't like to use that word lightly. I don't think I've ever been in love. But I know I'll know when I am, and I think it is a serious issue. I'm kind of an old soul.

"I have a cousin who used to tell me, you'll know you're in love when you care about the person you are with more than anything else, more than yourself; when they feel the same way about you and you have no idea why they do; and when you can't find the right words to say how you're feeling or you just can't understand why. I think that is what love is—when it's unimaginable to be away from the person, and you care about what makes them happy more than what makes you happy."

Clay was very honest with *Rolling Stone* when asked about his attitudes toward premarital sex. "My own personal position is that it's much more special to wait for the person who you're married to," although he invoked the Britney Spears rule when asked if he was still a virgin. "I watched a biography of Britney Spears on TV. In it, she said that she regrets ever saying anything about it. So, I hate to repeat myself, but I think it's much more special to wait for the person who you're married to."

Even if Aiken didn't have the emotional reference points to sell the heartbreak at the soul of the song, his voice was still powerful enough to make for a fine delivery. But Rickey Smith's "Endless Love" left the home audience unmoved. The next day, Smith expressed surprise he'd been ejected. "It was a little shocking," he said. "But, hey, I went out there and did my best. I have no complaints."

For the Bubels, hearing Clay sing in person in a professional venue was a special treat. So was meeting Clay's main rival, Ruben Studdard. Diane was surprised at how much Studdard's 6'4" height towered over her. She told the *Charlotte Observer,* "He really is a presence," referring to both his stature and his talent.

After the show ended, Clay took Diane and Emma out to dinner to catch up on each other's lives. One of the first questions Diane asked Clay was whether or not it was true that he and Carmen were dating. The rumor, flying on Clay Aiken sites all over the Internet, started after Clay and Carmen exchanged an obvious display of affection on one of the early episodes. Clay assured Diane there was no romance between them; Carmen had just wanted to make her sometime boyfriend jealous. According to Clay, while he liked Carmen, his affection for her was strictly platonic—he thought of her as a sister but nothing more.

Even if Clay had wanted to date someone, the rehearsal schedule would have made it difficult. As soon as one round was over, those who survived immediately turned their energies and attention to the following week's show, which required daily rehearsals. Plus, it could take up to eight hours to finish taping each week's promotional spots. "The demands that are made on everybody are staggering," acknowledged associate producer Patrick Lynn, which is why producers treated everyone to a day spa, a luxury Ruben particularly relished. According to the *Collegiate Standard*'s Wayne Cooper, Ruben said, "I took full advantage of the spa the other day. The pedicure was the bomb but the facial was good, too. We've been working so hard, it was great to have."

Having one performer in the house is usually enough for most families, but having a houseful of would-be pop stars would test the patience of even a saint, or in this case, Clay. Around the time the Bubels came to visit Clay, who shared a room above the three-car garage with Josh, Aiken was starting to feel the tension. He would later explain that being in the middle of a large group of people all used to being the center of attention was sucking the life out of him. "It was like, if I have to be around these people for one more minute, I'm going to kill them," he said. "It's a big house but not big enough!" His solution was to stay to himself, and almost avoid the others, until he could come to grips with the personalities of his *Idol* roommates. In typical fashion, Aiken's angst didn't last, and he was soon back to enjoying the experience of Casa de Idol.

The 8,000-square-foot house where the contestants lived during the competition was a multimillion-dollar seven-bedroom mansion nestled in Hollywood Hills. Their neighbors included *Will & Grace*'s Debra Messing, and Drew Barrymore. To ensure their privacy—and safety—there was a security gate and twenty-four-hour chaperones to keep an eye on the young performers. Compared to the others, Clay joked, "I kind of am the one here who's the goody-goody." And to make sure nobody strayed, there was "No alcohol; no smoking inside the house; a midnight curfew on singing; you have to clean up your own dishes; girls and guys in the common areas only."

Also staying at the house was Kristin Holt, who had been a contestant during the first season. Afterward, she had sent a tape in and producers hired her to be the official in-house correspondent. Among her revelations was that Ruben rarely missed his midnight snack, Josh couldn't cook, there were five different types of milk on the refrigerator shelf, and a number of the contestants swore by herbal lozenges imported from Sweden that tasted so bad they were called "greasy-oilies" but worked so well the house went through ten boxes a week. Then there were the perks, which included a personal chef who cooked twice a week, a workout room, a billiards table, a game room, and, most importantly, maid service. There was also a pool and hot tub, which Clay never went near because he suffers from extreme aquaphobia.

Not surprisingly, some of the antics smacked of frat house shenanigans, with Josh pulling practical jokes, like putting shaving cream in Ruben's bed (in return, Ruben hid Josh's shoes). All of the high jinks simply reflected the affection they had for one another.

On a typical evening, a visitor would find the guys hanging out on one side of the house at the pool table, where Ruben insisted there be a five-dollar kitty, and the girls primping on the other side of the house, hair dryers constantly blowing. "We spend a lot of time in the bathroom together getting ready," Kimberley Locke admitted. "We always ask for each other's opinion about what we are wearing."

Although everybody got along, inevitably some became closer friends than others. Trenyce and Kimberly Caldwell became so chummy that they'd wear each other's clothes and frequently go shopping together. Clay, Kimberley Locke, and Ruben were more homebodies and became the three amigos, with Clay and Kimberley sharing deep religious convictions. About the only time there were serious disagreements was when it came to selecting songs. As Lythgoe said, "Living together in the same house forces them to become friends. You can't live in a house with people you don't get on with."

But for all the pampering and the slumber-party atmosphere that went on for most of the week, typically Wednesday evenings were difficult for everyone because it meant someone had been cut, reminding them all how temporary their togetherness was. Watching a fellow contestant pack up could be an emotional experience. "It's just not fun on Wednesday," admitted Clay in a *Collegiate Standard* article. Charles Grigsby remembered that Clay helped him pack after he was eliminated on March 19. The group also made it a tradition to go out to dinner together every Wednesday so that they'd have the chance and the time to say goodbye the right way. Producer Lynn said it was truly family time. "Meals are our time to talk to each other. If you take a cell phone call, you have to pay a buck."

But for as bittersweet as it might have been to see a colleague go, come Thursday morning it was time to get back to work. However, it was during the week dedicated to Billy Joel that Clay learned firsthand the truism behind the show biz cliché "the show must go on."

It was widely known among the other contestants that Clay had several allergies, including coffee, chocolate, shellfish, and, of all things, mint. Shortly before the April 15 telecast, Aiken started coming down with hives and swelling. It turned out he had inadvertently eaten mint in a fruit salad he'd been munching on. Immediately producers called for medical attention, and Clay required several cortisone shots to suppress his allergic reaction.

Fortunately the treatment worked, and the audience was none the wiser when he performed "Tell Her About It," a song that gave Clay an opportunity to do something up-tempo. During his performance, he looked polished, wearing a pair of gray slacks, a T-shirt, and a sport coat.

Once, when asked by Suzanne Shoaf Ward what he used as motivation to rev himself up for his *American Idol* performances, Aiken denied really having specific motivation. "I don't have somebody that I want to sound like. I learn the song and I sing it. It's a lot simpler than what some reporters would like to make it. Why do I come across with such confidence? I don't know. I'm comfortable up there once I learn the song. But really, it's adrenaline. I get nervous backstage and then you hear *Clay Aiken* and then you walk out and you've got to do it. You have no other choice. I don't have the option to be nervous."

As he performed the Billy Joel standard, the audience got into the song, creating a nice energy. Clay's stage presence was clearly evolving, to the point where afterward Paula challenged him by saying she'd like to see him add some dance moves to his performance. Aiken responded by saying he was still working his way up to that. Ironically, the evening's guest host, Smokey Robinson, was never really known for cutting a rug on stage, but had made a career of crooning and smoothness. He wasn't bothered by Clay's limited mobility, calling the performance "terrific."

Simon said that while Clay sounded great, as usual, he preferred listening to him with his eyes closed so that he wouldn't have to watch Clay's facial expressions. It was these kinds of digs that once prompted Aiken to say, "I'm just gonna go out, sing my songs, have fun and expect Simon to say something mean."

But Clay could take comfort in knowing that three thousand miles away, 130 students were crowding into the UNCC student center to cheer him on. The local Fox News was there covering the pep rally, and aired signs that screamed, GO, CLAY, GO! Among the throng were some of his professors, the dean of the college, and some old friends. "I was looking through the message board on the American Idol Web site, and I was amazed at what people are saying about him," Amy Pusey told a *Charlotte Observer* reporter, recalling a posting that asked, "'Can anybody get me a date with him?' and 'He's *so* hot!' And I'm thinking, *My Clay?*"

Student Stacy Moses probably spoke for many of Clay's professors when she noted, "He would have been an excellent teacher. But he needs to follow his dream." Then she added, "He's our vanilla teddy bear."

Once again, America agreed and Clay was voted among the top performers. Caldwell wasn't so lucky, and to the surprise of many who thought it was time for Carmen to get the hook, Kimberly was sent packing, leaving just six contestants: Ruben, Carmen, Joshua, Trenyce, Clay, and Kimberley Locke.

But Carmen was living on borrowed time. The following week, which saluted songwriter Diane Warren, the teenager came to the end of her road. Although Clay was again voted among the top contestants, Simon seemed particularly peeved and puckish over Aiken's interpretation of "I Could Not Ask For More," which Warren originally wrote as a country song. Letting out a great sigh, Cowell snidely observed that Clay could make a great living as a "Broadway artist" but he wasn't what *American Idol* was all about. Then as a kicker he added, "Don't take this the wrong way, but I hate looking at you."

Typically, Clay absorbed the criticism without lashing back, in part because he was conscious of being watched by millions of people, including kids. "I come across as more meek than I really am."

When *Billboard*'s Fred Bronson asked Clay to compare the judges, another reason that Clay accepted Cowell's comments came to light. "Randy and Paula told you when they thought something was wrong. They didn't have any problems being constructively critical, but they were very supportive backstage. They were thrilled to see you and would give you a hug or talk to you and they were very honest. But they tempered it in a way that a family member would. 'I'm telling you this because I love you. . . . You could have done better.'"

Whereas, he said, Simon was like the wicked stepbrother. "He's an honest guy. He realizes he's the reason this show is so popular, but he doesn't take his persona too seriously. He doesn't want to hurt anybody's feelings. That's not his intention. He's going to tell the honest truth, and I think for that reason, Simon scared me while I was on the show." But, at the same time, Aiken admitted, "Simon probably made me work harder than anybody else, because I was never really worried about what Randy and Paula were going to say. I wouldn't second-guess myself, but I tried to second-guess Simon. Sometimes he'd give criticism that I could do something with. He's the one you don't want to tick off, but he's the one you want to make happy, then you work on it."

Call it tough Idol love. But if Cowell was riding Clay simply to challenge him to be the best he could be, his marine-type tactic was working, because as the show entered its final weeks, Clay had become the front-runner to win the competition. In the end, Aiken was about to learn that it truly wasn't whether you won or lost, but how you presented yourself to the American public that counted.

Chapter Ten

Down to the Wire

It was certainly enough to make Simon Cowell feel old. The April 29 *American Idol* episode featured music from the sixties, including songs by Neil Sedaka, a genuine pop music pioneer and legend among the Baby Boomer crowd. Sedaka also happened to be the guest celebrity judge. Right out of high school, Sedaka teamed with Howard Greenfield. Their careers quickly took off in 1958 after Connie Francis recorded their songs "Stupid Cupid" and "Where the Boys Are." A few years later Sedaka signed a recording contract, and in the 1960s he became one of the original pop idols with a string of hits cowritten with Greenfield that included "Calendar Girl," "Happy Birthday, Sweet Sixteen," and "Breaking Up Is Hard to Do." But by the late 1960s, after the British invasion led by the Beatles and Rolling Stones, Sedaka's style of music fell out of favor.

In the mid-1970s, Elton John brought Sedaka out of semi-obscurity by signing him to his Rocket record label and producing two best-selling albums, one of which included "Laughter in the Rain," which was a number one hit in America. In 1975, Sedaka rerecorded "Breaking Up Is Hard to Do" as a ballad, and it again reach number one. Around the same time, he and Greenfield wrote "Love Will Keep Us Together" for Captain and Tennille, which went on to win a Grammy Award for Record of the Year.

Although Sedaka had over forty years of hits, most of the young finalists had never even heard of the Hall of Fame songwriter/singer. As Sedaka noted, "My songs were written long before the *American Idol* contestants were even born." Soon, they would all be singing his songs.

With their numbers dwindling, contestants would perform two solo songs, and instead of the three with the least number of votes having to fight for survival, now just the bottom two would be on the hot seat.

Clay's first song was the very bouncy, very fluffy "Build Me Up Buttercup." As everyone in the theater and at home had come to expect, Clay's voice was strong and his pitch was perfect. It was clear the guy could sing, and all the judges responded accordingly, even Simon, who appeared more interested in figuring out what exactly *Buttercup* means. Ruben was similarly lauded after he sang the old Temptations hit "Ain't Too Proud to Beg."

For his second act, Aiken chose the ballad "Solitaire," a song he said he has "loved from high school." Clay thought one of the reasons the performance got such a positive reception from the audience was because, as he related to Fred Bronson, he went to the source. "I called Neil Sedaka and said, 'I want to know exactly what this man's thinking. Did he commit suicide or something at the end of the song?' I wasn't exactly sure what the motivation was. I wanted to know."

Sedaka was visibly moved by Clay's interpretation. "Bravo, Clay," he applauded. "I have lost my song forever to you." Sedaka also pointedly mentioned how much he'd love to work with Clay on an album and write songs for it. Perhaps feeling a bit territorial, since it would be Cowell's management company that would represent the ultimate winner, Simon heaped unaccustomed praise onto Clay, rating his performance "a 10." He also complimented Clay for being "one of the few people that can take criticism" and use it to improve.

Clay's mother was in the audience that night and waved a sign that read, AIRFARE $350; HOTEL $100 A NIGHT; SEEING MY SON, CLAY, BECOME THE NEXT AMERICAN IDOL: PRICELESS.

Probably most people watching the show assumed it would be Josh and Trenyce fighting for their *Idol* lives the following night, with Josh being shipped back to his base. So it was a stunning turn of events when Ryan Seacrest announced that those with the lowest number of votes were Trenyce and Ruben.

The judges acted as if someone had zapped their chairs with electricity. Studdard looked stumped by the indignity of it all. Josh had that my-life-just-passed-before-my-eyes glaze, and the judges were a swirl of confusion, dismay, and anger. Zap2it's Daniel Fienberg suggested Simon's ire came from fear of "what would happen if his label had to produce a whole album of country songs catered to Josh's half-octave range. Seriously, singing ability is subjective. Notes and lyrics are not subjective. . . . In his very limited comfort zone, he's quite acceptable, but outside of that zone, he's been genuinely inept." Fienberg went on to say, "Josh proponents should check out *Nashville Star,* where the talent would prove that Josh is a dilettante in that genre as well."

Paula lost her sunny disposition and announced that the thought of Ruben having to even entertain the possibility of elimination was "absolutely ridiculous." Randy chastised the home audience. "This is not happening. We're trying to find the best people in America to win this competition. That kid is brilliant up there. I don't know what y'all been hearing."

Simon also reminded the audience they had a responsibility to judge this properly, then felt compelled to stress, "At the end of the day we've given the public the right to vote and you have to respect their decisions."

After all the Sturm und Drang, Seacrest announced that it was time for Trenyce to hit the road. Everyone on stage looked relieved, none more so than Ruben. In analyzing why Ruben had been pushed to the brink, Zap2it's Fienberg explained it was probably a simple case of complacency. "Ruben's fans knew he was good, knew he was safe and didn't feel the need to vote in large numbers. . . . Josh's fans, on the other hand, knew that he deserved to get removed and voted in large numbers to keep him around well past his expiration date. Pity anybody who actually believes that Josh is a better singer than Ruben. Maybe this will be what Ruben needs to discover a higher gear and reclaim his briefly ceded position as favorite in this competition."

Of course not everyone agreed Ruben *was* the favorite. Aiken's fans, who by this time were organized enough to have given themselves the nickname Claymates, had mobilized and were campaigning for their Idol choice on the Internet in fan sites and chat rooms. Although he was aware of the support, Aiken tried to keep it in perspective, fearing "it might give a false sense of hope."

His hometown fans were also encouraging people to support Clay. News 14 Carolina tracked down Aiken's old friend Suzanne Lyczkowski from the A.E. Finley YMCA, who still referred to him as Gonzo, the nickname given to him at the Y during his time there as a counselor. "I counted. I think I've spent twenty hours voting for him. And I sent him an e-mail and said before the end of this thing I will have spent over an entire day voting for him." Lyczkowski said that while she had always known "Gonzo" had a talent for performing, "We never imagined that he would ever do something as big as this. We are so excited and so proud of him."

Lyczkowski had set up a fan site and reported that she had received thousands of pieces of fan mail. Clay mania was also creating some cottage industries. Raleigh's PKD Screen Printing, which had started selling Clay merchandise locally, was suddenly inundated with orders once news of it got out on the Internet. "We're probably doing 300 to 400 phone calls a day, and it's increasing every day," PKD owner Paulette Disbrow reported to News 14. "We've actually pulled in three people just to handle the phone calls." She added that part of the proceeds from the Clay Aiken T-shirts, CDs, and pendants they were selling would be donated to his favorite causes.

Among those rooting for Clay was his old roommate, Amy Pusey, who admitted in *Clay Aiken Unplugged* that it got more nerve-racking watching the show as the weeks counted down. But she also admitted worrying about what would happen to him if he didn't win.

"There is always the nervousness, how long this is going to last, and what is going to happen next, what is he going to fall back on if this does not work out. He has made the comment that he does feel jealous when he hears our classroom stories, but he is kind of afraid that when it is time . . . to go back to teach, . . . parents and students and others [will] not take him seriously as a teacher, as a Mr. Aiken."

She worried perhaps more about what would happen if he did win. "Clay has wonderful, wonderful fans but I do worry for him from what you hear about famous people. I am worried about him getting hurt by somebody or getting threatened. Just crazy things that can happen once people get famous. I think he is pretty careful with it. He has not done anything foolish. But it is such a huge step for Clay."

With the competition down to the final four, the national attention on Clay and the others was intense. What made the situation so bittersweet for Aiken was that on the one hand, he wanted to win, but on the other, he wanted Kimberley and Ruben, who had become close friends, to also do well. As he told the *Charlotte Observer* in early May, "I would absolutely love to be in the top three with Kim and Ruben. We all have a mutual respect for each other. I would absolutely say the two of them are my best friends here."

Beyond that, Aiken had to admit, "I would love to be in the top two, mainly because I want to be here to the end of the show."

Clay seemed to think that if he didn't win the competition outright, his days as a performer would be over, and he seemed at peace with that scenario. "I'm so much further than I thought I would be—just being here is absolutely amazing to me. If it's not meant to happen, I'm totally, totally happy with going back to being a teacher." But as long as he was in the competition, Clay was playing to win. *Charlotte Observer* journalist Leigh Dyer reported that Aiken and the others always voted for themselves after the Tuesday performance. "I check to make sure my line is working," he said, laughing.

Clay also became much more outspoken about how he was presented on the air. *Entertainment Weekly*'s Dave Karger reported how Aiken had put his foot down about what stylist he worked with. "There was a particular person who did my hair on the show," Clay recounted. "For a period afterward they said, 'Let's use some other people.' And I looked like a greased pig. It was horrible. So I finally picked a battle there and said, 'Listen, we're getting him from now on.'"

Wardrobe supervisor Miles Siggins said, "There are a few people who have changed a lot, and Clay's one of them." He went on to reveal to the *Charlotte Observer* that Clay had become a bit of a shoe lover and had "learned to match his shoes to his shirts." Clay would later admit to his mom that his favorite pair of shoes cost $200, an amount he would never have spent back home in Raleigh.

Because they were friends, the performers tended to blunt their ambitions with humor. When asked to rate themselves against the others, Studdard joked, "All I can say is, 205 beats 704," referring to his and Clay's respective hometown area codes. But in truth, they all felt blessed to even be in this position. "We've all won, just to get this far," Clay told *USA Today.* "Even the person who leaves this week—please, God, don't let it be me—is number 4 out of 70,000. . . . Every week I think I'm going home. It's a mathematical thing that somebody has to be the lowest, and so every week I think, *It's going to be the week.* I'm blessed to be around as long as I've been." Ruben agreed. "I'm going to make sure I take advantage of every moment," he said. "My goal was really to make the top thirty-two. God has blessed me to get above and beyond what I imagined."

Regardless of how the final voting turned out, the first week in May it was announced that Aiken, Studdard, and

Locke, along with other as of yet unnamed finalists, would participate in a thirty-nine-date North American tour. It would start July 8, 2003, in St. Paul, Minnesota, and end August 31 back in Anaheim, California. Plus, all the finalists were enjoying brisk record sales on their ensemble recording of Lee Greenwood's "God Bless the U.S.A." So even as the series' second season prepared to come to a close, there would be life after *Idol* for Clay even if he didn't win.

Without question, Clay's closest friend during the competition had become Kimberley Locke, who revealed that she and Clay were seriously considering renting a house together in Los Angeles after the show ended. "I love Clay," she told the *Observer.* "He's very much like me. He's very genuine." And she trusted him so much, it was to him she would go for advice on her songs. "I always go to Clay because I know he's going to tell me the truth."

Others on *American Idol* marveled at how much Clay had matured as a performer and how much more sophisticated he had become as far as style and appearance. Producer Lythgoe observed, "When he first walked in, let's face it, he looked like he had two satellite dishes growing out of his head." To which Clay retorted, "I know that I've got big ears and a big forehead and that my hair sticks up. But I'm happy with myself. I'm not necessarily trying to win a beauty pageant here."

Clay and the others also had to deal with the sometimes disconcerting experience of being recognized wherever they went. Although Aiken was never a drinker, back home in North Carolina he might occasionally have a beer or glass of wine with dinner. But when he became aware that his every move was being watched and scrutinized, he stopped drinking even that much. "I don't think that's an example I want to set for somebody—not if I want to be the American Idol," he said.

As the competition got down to its final weeks, the importance of the song selection seemed magnified. In an interview with *Billboard*'s Fred Bronson, who had been an avid supporter from the beginning, Clay would later give credit to *Idol*'s music supervisor Susan Slamer, vocal coach Debra Byrd, and Michael Orland, the pianist and arranger.

"If I had a question, I could call Byrd at home. I could ask this and that, and then she'd come in and we'd rehearse it. She would have me rehearse with a . . . water bottle in front of her in a room downstairs in the mansion.

"Michael Orland . . . was often the person whose opinion I sought when making a final decision on which song to sing. He really served as a parental figure throughout the season. He was always one of the most supportive of all in terms of providing encouragement and keeping things lighthearted. He's one of the funniest people I know.

"Susan Slamer, I think, has the entire catalog of every songwriter in the world in her head. She was probably the hardest-working person on the show in terms of the amount of sweat and tears she put in to the show and the contestants. I can't think of a better person for the job that she has. Not only does she have an amazing knowledge of music, but she has a visible and contagious love for it." Aiken said Slamer also doubled as den mother to the group. "She was probably the easiest person to tell your frustrations to, and she gave so selflessly of her time even outside of normal work hours."

As the excitement over who would be the next *American Idol* grew, Simon Cowell contrasted the response of Americans to the finalists with how the British public had reacted to its *Pop Idol* contestants. "If you would have asked me what I thought of America before I came over here, I would have used the word *corny.* And then you come over here and you find that it's not corny at all. British people are very cynical, they cannot bear someone else's success. Americans embrace other people's success. Everything in America is larger than life."

One thing Simon was less complimentary about in *USA Today* was how having celebrity judges was working out. "I personally find it a bit insulting having celebrity judges on the show. To me, it's our role and nobody else's to judge these kids, because we've chosen them from the beginning." Nigel Lythgoe shrugged off the complaint and quipped, "The only time he's happy to be next to anyone is when he's leaning against a mirror."

But Cowell disagreed and made it clear that part of the success of *Idol* was based on the disparate personalities of the judges. "If you had three people on the panel who were like me, it would be awful; it would just be gratuitous, who could come up with the best insult. Part of its appeal is that we are so different."

Despite the weekly dramas and occasional upsets with who got voted off, Simon tended to look at the big picture. "You don't want a situation you had last year, where the best or second-best singer gets kicked out before she has a chance to make the finals," he said, clearly referring to the first year when Tamyra Gray was voted off, leaving Kelly Clarkson to vie with an overmatched Justin Guarini for the title. "The audience short-changed themselves a little bit and missed the chance to see a great final. It was a bit like a heavyweight taking on a lightweight, and that's a problem. That's not being disrespectful to Justin; he'll be the first to admit Tamyra was a better singer."

He also said, "So as long as we've got two good finalists, I don't really care. Whoever comes in third, fourth or fifth isn't really a major issue to me as long as the two I like make the finals. And I think the best two are Ruben and Clay. The best thing that's come out of this competition by far is the fact that the two front-runners are so non-typical music business, and that in a way is a good thing. It's responding to what the public is saying: that we want something different."

They certainly got something different from Clay on the next episode, which featured Robin Gibb as guest judge to watch the final four sing songs made famous by the Bee Gees. As if there weren't enough pressure already, the rehearsals were marked by a complication producers did not want to see—both Josh and Clay announced they wanted to sing "To Love Somebody." The producers tried to get one of them to change songs. Clay stood his ground because he says the only rule given to the competitors that week was that they had to choose one ballad and one up-tempo song. "If my gut says sing 'To Love Somebody,' I'm singing 'To Love Somebody.' Josh is going to sing it too, but I'm not going to second-guess myself and try to flip-flop on what I want, so I'm going to sing it," he explained later to the *Charlotte Observer.* Finally Lythgoe gave in, telling Josh and Clay, "Okay, if you two want to do it, if you want to go up against each other, then go for it."

Paula, Randy, and Robin uniformly give all the competitors praise and kudos for their songs. Simon, on the other hand, told Josh that he shouted "Jive Talkin'," and he got booed for telling Kimberley she was sweet but ordinary and not as good as he had seen her in the past. He praised Ruben, then surprised Clay by saying Clay had done such a good job, he thought he'd be the next American Idol. Considering Clay had once commented, "Getting a compliment from Simon is like getting water out of a rock," his surprise and pleasure were obvious.

However, all that goodwill abruptly dispersed after Clay performed his next song, "Grease." Not only did Aiken dude it up by wearing a red jacket and matching red shoes, he actually incorporated a few dance moves. Although he thought "Grease" was "one of my best vocal performances," he'd later admit that maybe the dance moves hadn't been such a good idea. Although Paula was especially pleased to see Clay be more physically expressive, Simon was appalled. "Everything about that was horrible," he told Clay, then announced to the booing audience, "He had a great performance then threw everything away with that one." Not that Cowell was insinuating that Clay should get voted off, but that Clay might have given Ruben the edge in what Simon's mind was a two-man race.

Even though Fox would have loved to make the results show more dramatic, nobody was surprised when Josh was finally voted off. Simon, still peeved over Trenyce's premature departure, commented that Josh should have been ousted the week before and that this week it should have been Kimberley.

But as they always say on the show, you never know. And with three weeks remaining, it was the three amigos left standing. As a reward for their perseverance, and to better promote the final three shows, producers arranged for the three finalists to fly back and visit their respective hometowns. And what a homecoming it would be for Clay.

Chapter Eleven

Homecoming King

You know it's national news when Oprah Winfrey gets interested. The talk-show hostess was in Hollywood to tape a segment for her show that would take a behind-the-scenes look at *American Idol 2*. Participating in the show, which was taped right after the three finalists were announced, were the three judges; Kelly Clarkson, who was there to promote her new single; and Locke, Studdard, and Aiken. Also included were Josh Gracin, who admitted he was "very, very relieved" after being eliminated from the competition just minutes earlier, and Faye Parker. Immediately after the taping was over, Clay and his mother boarded a plane for Raleigh.

When Clay had left North Carolina for Hollywood after making the cut for the final thirty-two, he had been a mostly anonymous college student. When he returned for a whirlwind two-day visit after making it to the final three, he was a full-blown national celebrity and local hero.

"It's amazingly overwhelming," he acknowledged to the *Herald-Sun*. "It still hasn't settled in with me. I was just here two months ago and I was walking down the street and nobody knew me. We went to the bank today and people were running outside because they recognized me. And we were driving through the teller. It's hard to let it soak in at this point. But it's very humbling and somehow, I don't feel very worthy of it."

Running on a lot of adrenaline and very little sleep, Aiken stopped first for a photo-op with Governor Mike Easley, who asked Clay to sing "On the Wings of Love."

Knowing Aiken was a James Taylor fan, Easley presented him with a photograph taken during the dedication of the

James Taylor Bridge over Morgan Creek. Clay thanked him and then added, "I want a bridge." Without missing a beat, Easley responded, "When you win it all, you'll get your bridge. . . . It might be a small one."

The governor then praised both Clay's *Idol* success and the work he had done with special needs children at the local YMCA. "You're making us proud. It says a lot about North Carolina values."

Clay's next stop was going back home to what was supposed to be an invitation-only lunch of about thirty friends and family. His mom had been deeply moved and grateful when a group of fans from Reston, Virginia, who had never met Clay or anyone in his family, paid to have her yard landscaped before *American Idol*'s producers showed up to tape a "back at home" segment that would air on the following week's performance show. They knew Faye's husband had died a year earlier and that she didn't have anyone to help her tend the yard. Clay's longtime friend Frances Wilson said, "I realized that Clay now belongs to the world, and not to his mom or his friends here in Raleigh anymore."

Later that afternoon, Clay was on the move again, this time to visit the A.E. Finley YMCA, where he was reunited with Suzanne Lyczkowski, who runs the YMCA's after-school program. Lyczkowski thanked Clay for mentioning the YMCA's program during his performances, because the publicity had helped raise $2,000 toward camp scholarships for underprivileged children. Aiken was self-effacing. "There have been so many people who have supported the Y simply because they've heard my name associated with it, and that's humbling," he admitted to the Associated Press.

But what Aiken didn't tell reporters was how he'd been kind to one of his former campers, Robert Nelson. A month earlier Robert had fallen and suffered such a severe cut on his leg that it left him confined to a wheelchair. The wound was so deep it actually went to the bone. Hoping that Clay might send Robert a get-well card, some of his old friends from the

Getty Images

Clay's warm personality and quick wit has made him a popular guest on television shows. Here he performs a song from his *Measure of a Man* album on *The Tonight Show with Jay Leno.*

Getty Images

Aiken reunites with some old *American Idol* friends at the 31st Annual American Music Awards, which was held in November 2003 at the Shrine Auditorium in Los Angeles. In the top photo Clay and Ruben Studdard clown around after an afternoon rehearsal and show off their *TV Guide* covers. In the bottom photo, Paula Abdul congratulates Clay on taking home the Fans' Choice Award.

WireImage

Getty Images

Clay interacts with fans during an appearance on MTV's *Total Request Live.* He displayed some of his well-known sense of humor by helping mold a clay figurine of Christina Aguilera.

Getty Images

While out raising money for the Bubel/Aiken Foundation, Clay is presented with a framed cover of his *Rolling Stone* issue, which was one of the magazine's best-selling issues in 2003.

Just days after being named *American Idol's* runner-up, Clay joined Ruben for a whirlwind press tour of New York City. Among his many appearances was one on the *Today Show*, which films at famed Rockefeller Center. Here Clay is shown passing by fans on his way into the building.

Getty Images

Clay shares a laugh with reporters during a visit to Washington, D.C., to promote the American Film Institute Screen Education Center.

AP Wideworld Photos

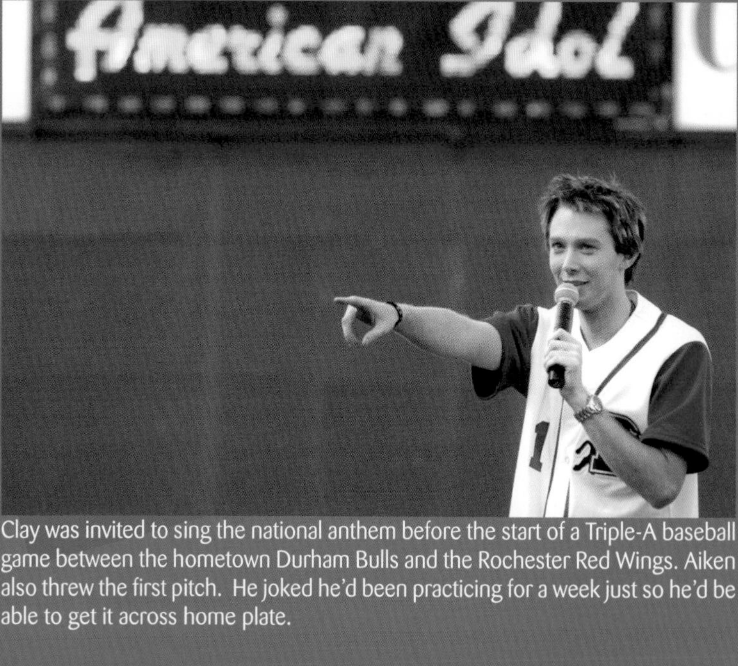

Clay was invited to sing the national anthem before the start of a Triple-A baseball game between the hometown Durham Bulls and the Rochester Red Wings. Aiken also threw the first pitch. He joked he'd been practicing for a week just so he'd be able to get it across home plate.

AP Wideworld Photos

During a visit back home to Raleigh the week before the *American Idol* finale, Aiken appeared at a press conference with North Carolina governor Mike Easley. Clay laughs when Easley tells him he needs to dance more while performing.

Getty Images

A week after the *American Idol* finale, Ruben and Clay performed in front of frenzied fans at Zootopia, a concert sponsored by New York radio station Z100.

Getty Images

During a break from their Independent Tour, Clay and Kelly Clarkson get up close and personal with a beluga whale at SeaWorld San Diego. Aiken said it was great having someone to tour with "to bounce ideas off of and to keep me sane."

Fitzroy Barrett/Globe Photos

Clay poses for photographers backstage at the American Music Awards, where he won Fans' Choice. During his acceptance speech, Clay joked he was overwhelmed by the honor because "I'm not used to winning anything; I'm kinda used to second place."

Getty Images

American Idol 2's twelve finalists pose for a group shot during an event sponsored by the Academy of Television Arts & Sciences. Originally voted off from his group of eight, Clay made it back to the finals after fans at home voted him back in.

AP Wideworld Photos

Clay gives it his all with this performance during the *American Idol 2* finale.

Getty Images

Clay's going to Disney World! Clay takes a spin at the Tomorrowland Indy Speedway with YMCA coordinator Kristy Hall.

Despite finding an unexpected career as a pop idol, teaching remains one of Aiken's passions. At the DisneyHAND Teacher Awards, Clay reunited with his former teachers Patsy Stone (l) and Mary Propes (r).

WireImage

AP Wideworld Photos

After completing an independent study project that led to the formation of the Bubel/Aiken Foundation, Clay earned enough credits to graduate in December 2003 with a degree in special education. After receiving his diploma, Aiken spoke to his fellow graduates about the importance of making a difference in people's lives.

Getty Images

Clay became a fan favorite during *American Idol 2* because of his powerful voice and down-home charm. When the final votes were tallied, Ruben Studdard won by less than one percent of the 24 million votes cast.

Getty Images

Clay chats with Jay Leno while promoting *Measure of a Man.*

Alec Michael/Globe Photos

Clay and his mom, Faye Parker. Even when he was a small child, Faye says she knew God had blessed her son with the gift of song. Clay's success has become a family affair, with Faye and Aiken's younger brother Brett handling all Clay's fan mail.

WireImage

Clay shows off his ice-skating skills while performing during an intermission of a professional hockey game between the Carolina Hurricanes and the Dallas Stars at the RBC Center in his hometown of Raleigh.

Getty Images

Just boyish good looks!

Clay shows his support for kids everywhere at a World's Children Day celebration along with Ronald McDonald (r) and fellow singer Jessica Simpson (c). Aiken's message is that children will thrive as long as they have love, respect, and opportunity.

Getty Images

Getty Images

American Dream!

YMCA called to tell Clay about the young boy's condition. Robert's mother, Robin, said she was shocked when the phone rang and it turned out to be Clay calling from Hollywood. "My husband took the phone call and was floored himself," she said. "I was thrilled. It was great for Robert. He was grinning from ear to ear."

It had been an emotional day for Clay, but it still wasn't over. That evening he was scheduled to throw out the opening pitch at a Durham Bulls game. The Bulls are the Triple-A team for the Tampa Bay Devil Rays. That night's game was a sellout, with frenzied fans waiting to greet Aiken. In true star style, Clay arrived via helicopter, which landed right on the field as the *American Idol* theme song blared over the loudspeakers. "This has been an amazing journey," he told the crowd, "and I have all of you to thank for it."

When it came time to throw the first pitch, Aiken warned the fans that his pitching skills lacked. "I'm not an athlete, so I need y'all to pray now that this ball gets all the way over to home." Clay managed to throw the ball over the plate, then led the stadium in the national anthem, singing it a cappella.

While in Durham, Clay spent some time with a reporter from the *Herald-Sun,* who asked if Clay had any plans past the end of the show. "It's kind of self-explanatory if I win," he answered. "But, if I don't win, it's an opportunity for a door to open. If this is what God wants for me to do, then those doors will open and it will happen for me. So I'm not going to be stressed out anymore. If I go this week, fine. If I don't make it to the final, that means my two best friends are in the final and I'm fine to go back to teaching. I'm very happy doing what I was doing before this started. I've auditioned enough. I can't go and do any more."

Although Clay talked of returning to teaching, it seemed unlikely. Bolstering that impression was Aiken's admission that he was already making arrangements to stay in L.A. regardless of the outcome. "Kim Locke and [I] have discussed possibly moving out, if the right doors are open. In my long-term goal, I want to live here," Clay said; still he listed the downsides of life in L.A: "The traffic is horrible. The people can be kinda nuts. The food has avocado on it everywhere you go. I don't dislike L.A. The weather is nice, but it's always the same. I love seasons. I like snow. I like the leaves to change color. If I lived in Raleigh I'd get all of that in the same yard. But you really can't have a career in Raleigh in this industry."

Aiken claimed he wasn't going to do anything different than he had been to prepare for the next show, and he also expressed respect for the job the judges were doing. "All of them have a very difficult job to do. Especially now. We're down to, in my opinion, two of the top talents in the country and me. I don't understand how they can differentiate. It's not about who is better anymore. It's about the style that the public likes. And the judges are really just giving their opinions at this point."

Clay said each of the judges has his or her own style, but that they all have valuable insight to offer. "Randy is a very constructively critical person. I appreciate the fact that he's honest with you but he tempers it with a little kindness. Paula is the artist. She's very supportive. She can be honest when she needs to. She told me I needed to dance some more, which I bet she's regretting now. But she's the nurturer. Simon is brutally honest. And I like him as a person. But he's a very brutally honest person."

Ironically, Cowell commented that he'd been blasted by the British, who felt he had toned down his criticisms for the second season. "I think they want me to carry an Uzi out on stage, or something." He sighed, then admitted it was possible he was less harsh, but only because "the contestants were more talented," giving him less to complain about.

Before heading back to California, Aiken made one unpublicized stop in Charlotte to visit Mike Bubel at school. After spending time with him, Aiken told a reporter the reunion had been "bittersweet," because even though Mike recognized him, he was unable to talk. Even so, Clay said, "It was really great to see him; he's made so much progress. It makes me a little sad to know that I wasn't a part of it and that I didn't get to see it happen."

Mike's mother was hopeful Clay's popularity would prompt more people to give time and money toward causes benefiting children with disabilities. "I hope there will be a trickle effect," she said.

Shortly after saying goodbye to the Bubels, Clay was on his way back to Los Angeles. Normally, this would be when the finalists would be immersed in the all-important song selection process. This week, producers had a twist for them. Each of them would sing three songs, but the contestant would get to choose only one of them. The judges would pick a second song for each, and the third song would be picked at random from a fishbowl full of slips of paper with songs on them.

Clay explained to Leigh Dyer that Nigel Lythgoe had selected songs he preferred to hear them sing. "Ruben had some R&B stuff Nigel liked to hear. He loved diva songs from Kim Locke, and with me, he called me a crooner from the very beginning of the show."

Kimberley chose "Band of Gold" from the fishbowl; the song on Ruben's slip of paper was "Signed, Sealed, Delivered;" and Clay picked "Vincent" which he later said was Lythgoe's favorite song. Unfortunately for Aiken, none of the judges was impressed with either the song or Clay's performance of it, which wasn't helped by his forgetting some of the words. While Locke and Studdard both received three thumbs up for their random songs, not even Paula pretended to approve of Clay's, saying it wasn't his best performance. Simon summed it up as "dreary" but put it off as possibly just a case of nerves.

Next up were the judges' choice songs, which were presumably chosen to showcase each of the contestants' strengths. Randy told the audience that Kimberley would be singing Burt Bacharach's "Anyone Who Had a Heart." Despite a weak beginning, Kim ended strong. Randy was pleased,

Paula compared her to Sarah Hughes, and Simon called it a safe performance but let it be known he was not blown away.

Simon presented Ruben's song, "Smile," which Ruben performed with seeming ease. Randy, again, was pleased. Paula complimented Studdard by saying he warmed everyone's heart, and Simon deemed it a job well done.

Clay knew there wasn't much room for error, so when it was time for him to sing the song chosen by the judges, "Mack the Knife," he went for it. Simon spoke for them all when he called the performance brilliant and told Clay he had pulled himself back in contention.

The last round was each singer's choice; producers suggested they pick a song relating to an idol of their own. Locke chose Natalie Cole's "Inseparable," which played up her vocal strengths much more than the judges' pick had. The audience loved it and so did the judges, with Simon commenting that all three of the finalists were worthy of going on to the next round.

Ruben was up next and sang Peabo Bryson's "If Ever You're In My Arms Again." The judges had a hard time coming up with any new superlatives to describe Ruben, so they applauded his talent and moved on to Clay.

For his final turn, Clay chose "Unchained Melody," which happened to be his mother's favorite song. Paula pronounced it the best performance of the competition, and although they were both complimentary, Randy and Simon were more muted in their praise.

Now the contestants had to wait twenty-four hours before finding out what America had decided.

After suffering through a results show that was agonizingly full of filler, the three contestants were brought to center stage. Ryan Seacrest announced that of the 19 million votes cast, there was only a 4 percent differential between the one with the fewest votes and the others. Without a lot of fanfare, Seacrest simply told Kimberley she was going home.

It seemed almost cruel to make her stand there and watch the traditional montage rather than letting her go to absorb the loss. Although Clay and Ruben were undoubtedly thrilled to be the two finalists, both looked upset for their friend.

Clay was so emotional that once he got backstage, he broke down in tears. A *Newsweek* reporter wanting to interview him had to wait several minutes. Staying true to form, when Simon walked by and heard Clay was crying, he quipped that they were probably tears of relief that Kimberley had been voted off and not him.

As had to be expected by this point, Locke's departure didn't come without its own share of controversy. A PR Newswire release recounted how two *Newsweek* reporters were claiming that during a rehearsal before the May 13 show, Simon Cowell had been overheard saying, "We have a problem. I want Ruben to be in the final two, and Kimberley just had a great rehearsal."

The reporters claimed that even though they felt Locke out-sang Studdard during the broadcast, Cowell craftily limited his praise for her and heaped it instead on Ruben, hoping to subtly sway the viewers. Simon admitted as much to Marc Peyser and Sean M. Smith. "When there's only three left, you are going to be slightly tactical. What you're trying to do, if you can, is to tell the audience who you want to be in the final. You're not getting accurate judging. You're not."

Locke would later claim in *Newsweek,* "The judges play to who they want to win. I believe they want Ruben. Simon says that every opportunity he gets."

When asked who they thought would win, Ruben and Clay expressed hesitant optimism. "I don't know, man." Ruben shrugged. "Hopefully it will be me." Clay agreed. "I really don't know but I could not be in better company." Despite Locke's impression, Cowell actually predicted Clay would win the competition "by a whisker. But I could be wrong."

The answer was just a week away.

Chapter Twelve

And the Winner Is . . .

After the elimination show, once the initial wave of emotion passed, Kimberley Locke regained her composure and in some ways seemed happier than the two finalists. "I'm just happy that we all got this far," Locke said as everyone mingled backstage. "It's a great jump-start for my career."

Plus, there was little time to dwell. Kimberley, Clay, and Ruben had to focus, because as soon as the broadcast ended, producers were going to start taping an *American Idol* special edition. It would be broadcast the following Monday as part of an *Idol* blitz that would culminate in the crowning of the new winner.

As it began to sink in just what he had accomplished, Clay admitted to *USA Today* that he was thrilled. "I got chills looking at the final last year. I'm just coming to the realization that that's going to be me next week. Right now it's very emotional. On the one hand, one of my best friends has to go home. On the other, I'm completely moved that I'm still here."

Studdard was typically low-key. "I thank God for the opportunity. I'm glad people are enjoying what I'm doing." He looked around, then added, "It's good to see everybody backstage, but it's sad to see everybody go. It's heart-wrenching, man, but it's just the name of the game."

It seemed as if the entire country was abuzz over who would be crowned the next American Idol. There was only a 2 percent differential between Clay and Ruben in the last vote, although nobody would say who had the lead. As fans for the respective performers sought to mobilize votes, the two finalists themselves tried to downplay the drama at a press conference arranged by Fox.

"I don't feel like I'm going up against Ruben," Clay said. "He and I have been close for a long time and I don't feel like really at this point it's a competition about who is better. We're both here because we've proven, to some extent, that we're good at what we do."

Aiken also noted that he and Studdard were fortunate to have tried out the second year instead of the first. "Last year, I don't think any of the three of us would have made the top thirty-two based on the way they were doing things," Clay said, including Locke in his observation. "It was a big image thing last year. They let people through based on how they looked on last season's show." Asked if he had any intention of changing strategies for the final show to downplay what Simon criticized as his "Broadway" tendencies, Clay shook his head. "I guess whatever it is that I'm doing now has worked for me so far with 27 million viewers, so hopefully it would be successful."

The two friends also maintained that they would be at peace regardless of the final tally. "Of course I want to win, but if not, I'm number two," Clay reasoned. "What comes out of this is what God wants to happen. I totally rely on him to put me where he wants to put me and he did that. I never would have auditioned for something like this. He allowed this to happen to me. I never in my life would have put myself in the top ten, much less in the final. If he wants me to win, then I'll win. If he wants me to come in second place, then I'll come in second place."

Ruben agreed. "God gives certain people favor, and me and Clay are just very fortunate."

Both believed the contest was going to be extremely close. "I could not pick between Ruben and me," Clay said, then laughed. "Oh, yeah, I could. I'd pick me!" His honesty over his desire to win prompted Simon to later say Clay was "the most ambitious that I've met in this whole competition."

Clay also candidly admitted that being in the spotlight can be addictive. "To see my name in lights has never really been a dream of mine. But I'll be honest, when I got to the *X-Men* premiere, and everyone's looking at me, and when I go home and I'm on the front page of both the papers, there is a little bit of me that doesn't want it to stop. After you've finally seen how cool it can be, it is kind of contagious."

It wasn't just the finalists who found themselves in the limelight. Faye Parker had become a celebrity in her own right back in North Carolina. She was invited to do radio interviews and was even stopped on the street for autographs, which Clay said she signed, "Clay's mom."

Raleigh mayor Charles Meeker named May 16 as Clay Aiken Day and presented the proclamation to Faye at a ceremony heavily attended by enthusiastic Clay fans. She was obviously touched by the outpouring of encouragement and affection. "I really just want to say thank you again to all of Raleigh and all of North Carolina for the support that they've given Clayton, because this has been a wonderful experience for him," she said. As an added bonus, the city honored her as well by planting a red sunset maple tree in her name at Buffaloe Road Park.

When asked her feelings about Clay's chances, she left it to a higher power. "Whatever God wants to happen is going to happen, and I think [Clay has] gone a long way and he's only gotten there because the fans put him there," she said. "It's their votes that count. I love them for it and I love my friends for standing by me."

But what was *American Idol* without some controversy? The week before the final episode, which would determine the winner, a Texas man filed a federal lawsuit against the producers of the show, claiming they had ripped off his idea. Harry Keane, Jr.—producer and racecar driver—claimed he had originally developed the concept for a show called *American Idol* back in 1994. Keane said his original concept called for national auditions, a thirteen-week television show with celebrity judges that would air two to three times a week and would have viewers voting on twenty contestants either via the phone or Internet. He claimed he had copyrighted the idea and had drawings made for how the show would look. Keane also claimed he had sent a proposal of his idea to FremantleMedia, which, along with Simon Fuller, was producing *American Idol.* FremantleMedia had also produced *Pop Idol,* the British version of the show.

Keane was asking a federal judge to impose a temporary restraining order that would keep the show off the air. He was also asking for damages—to the tune of $300 million—against Fox and FremantleMedia.

Several things immediately stood out about the lawsuit. First, no one can copyright an idea. A person can copyright a script, a book, or a song, but ideas themselves are not protected under U.S. copyright law. Second, back in 1994 the Internet had only just started to be a blip on the U.S. consumer radar screen, so it seemed somewhat dubious that anyone would have made Internet voting a centerpiece of a television series pitch. Then there was the detail that in 1994, FremantleMedia didn't exist. The company was previously known as Pearson Television, which wasn't founded until 1995.

Keane's attorney, Ryan Bormaster, was asked why Keane was only now filing the lawsuit, just a week before the Clay-Ruben showdown, considering *American Idol* had been airing in the U.S. for two years and *Pop Idol* had been a hit in the UK prior to that. The lawyer said Keane was unaware of the British version and that it had taken him this long to get his paperwork together to file suit against the American version.

"The claim he is making is ridiculous, and the lawsuit is ridiculous," a network spokesman said. A U.S. District Court judge in Houston agreed. He denied Keane's request the Friday prior to the season-two finale and effectively tossed the lawsuit out.

In the days leading up to the May 20 competition, various newspapers and organizations conducted informal polls to see who America would choose, making the competition seem more like a presidential race than a talent show. *USA Today* reported that those in the business seemed to be rooting for Studdard. "Everyone here is voting for Ruben," said Melinda Bell, vice president of Johnny Wright Entertainment Group, which represented Britney Spears and numerous boy bands such as 'NSYNC and the Backstreet Boys. "He has the showmanship and the voice, but also something else that is marketable and is not around right now. Name one person around now who has that Luther Vandross quality, that smooth voice and demeanor. No one else can compete."

And indeed, the cynics among us suspected that the reason Simon Cowell was pushing for Ruben is because he believed the soulful singer from Birmingham, Alabama, would be easier to market than Clay, who would fall in the cracks between several genres.

After conducting a poll that resulted in over 25,000 votes, online entertainment site Zap2it.com said that Clay had won by a relative landslide, taking 56.9 percent of the vote, compared to Ruben's 43.1 percent. Perhaps that was because Clay's fans seemed to be much more Internet-organized than Ruben's. In the end, all it confirmed was how close a race it was going to be.

For the final episode, the format would be slightly different than the first year's finale. Instead of Aiken and Studdard singing the same songs in a "compare and contrast" presentation, they would each sing three songs with no overlap. And to better give it that big extravaganza feel, the show would be broadcast from the Universal Amphitheater.

Despite the hype and the genuine interest in the show, it's doubtful that either Clay or Ruben changed anyone's mind with their last performance, because although both were good, they both also showed signs of feeling the pressure, which prevented either from being truly spectacular overall. Both had sung better on other nights, both had been more consistent in other rounds. This vocal duel was primarily a showcase, because it would really be the cumulative impressions generated over the past three months that viewers at home would be voting on.

On the basis of a coin toss, Ruben opened the show. He chose "A House Is Not a Home" and sounded fine. Clay countered with the original song "This Is the Night," after which Simon told him he could do better.

Ruben's next song was John Lennon's "Imagine," of which Zap2it's Fienberg observed, "This song has been covered so many times that Ruben has to struggle to give it his own imprint. His is a nice, but hardly remarkable, version notable mostly for Ruben's attempt to eschew his normal smile. Randy calls it nice. Paula doesn't say anything. Simon says it was risky, but that Ruben pulled it off."

Aiken then served up Paul McCartney's "Here, There and Everywhere." Randy and Paula gave it high marks, while Cowell hoped both contestants had just been saving the best for last.

Ruben's final song, "Flying Without Wings," prompted Paula Abdul to join the audience in waving their arms back and forth. Afterward she equated it to a religious experience. In this case, Simon agreed and said he was pleased that Ruben had pulled through.

For his last at-bat, Clay sang "Bridge Over Troubled Water." Using the song to emphasize his vocal strengths, he finished to a standing ovation. Simon observed that despite being off earlier in the evening, with that performance, Clay just might have won himself the title.

As the show closed, the camera caught Ruben saying something to Clay. Some of the more zealous of Clay's fans convinced themselves that Studdard was telling Clay he thought Aiken had the title won. But the television show *Ex-*

tra put those ambitious thoughts to rest by revealing that Ruben said, "Look at those women!" referring to the ladies in the audience waving pro-Clay signs. "I was like, dawg! Look at all them girls screaming for you! And, they were looking *good*!"

The only thing left to do was to wait—and to spend the next twenty-four hours preparing for the season finale. Fox was stretching the show into a two-hour marathon filled with a variety of time-killing features, skits, and performances. During the show, RCA Music Group chairman Clive Davis, who would be working with the winner on his album, presented Kelly Clarkson with a Recording Industry Association of America platinum award for her album *Thankful,* which had debuted at number one on the Billboard 200 when released the month before, in April.

By the time Ryan Seacrest was ready to announce the winner, almost 40 million people were watching, which is a bigger audience than watched the Academy Awards. According to SBC Communications, the company logged more than 24 million phone calls Tuesday evening once the voting was opened, an 80 percent increase in call volume compared to an average weeknight.

In what would become the focal point of scrutiny over the fairness and accuracy of the vote, Seacrest wound up giving three different figures for how many votes separated Clay and Ruben. In the first half hour of the broadcast, he said there was a difference of only 13,000. But when he revealed the decision, it had dwindled to a mere 1,300, meaning the runner-up had received 49.72 percent of the ballots, compared to 50.28 for the winner, who was . . . Ruben Studdard.

Zap2it's Daniel Fienberg called Clay "a spectacularly graceful loser" who "led the crowd in chants of *Ruben! Ruben!*"

Although Aiken joked, "I'm going to beat him up later for stealing my title," he'd later say during an interview with New York radio station Z100 that there was no crushing sense of disappointment after hearing the results. "I didn't really feel much, and most people don't believe me when I say that it was not a humongous deal to me. We had both prepared ourselves for either outcome. We were both just thrilled to be in the top two. Tuesday night right before we both went out to sing you know, Ruben said, 'Look at this. The two most unlikely people to be in the top two. And here we are.'"

So when Ryan read Ruben's name, Aiken assured *TV Guide* the expression on his face "was really a look of indifference. Winning the competition was simply icing; it wasn't something that we necessarily had to have. We were both very happy with being where we were."

The prize Ruben won was a recording contract with Clive Davis on RCA's J Records label. But the biggest surprise came when Simon announced that Davis had agreed to oversee albums for *both* Clay and Ruben, and that their albums would be released on the same day. Although there was certainly a benefit in having the bragging rights of being crowned the next American Idol and the monetary prize that went with it, suddenly even the runner-up was a winner. Aiken was shocked. "That's the first time I knew I was going to be signed to RCA. I was told right then."

Tom Ennis from 19 Entertainment said that originally, they were only going to sign the winner. "But that all changed when we saw the results of the voting were so close," he explained. "We were blown away by Clay's talent and the fact that he appeals to millions of people. We knew we had to sign him."

In a very real way, the competition had extended beyond Fox, prompting Simon to say the *real* competition would be on the charts and the first round would begin June 3, when Aiken's and Studdard's singles would be released. Although the album was unexpected for Aiken, he had known there would be a single.

Immediately after Trenyce had been voted off, Josh Gracin, Kim Locke, Ruben, and Clay had had a meeting with Clive

Davis at the Beverly Hills Hotel. Davis told them that there were going to be two different singles. "Instead of both finalists singing the same song like on the first season, they were going to have one finalist sing one song and one finalist sing the other song," Clay explained in *Billboard*. "One of the reasons they did that was because two people could have a single, and the other reason was that way you could really match each person's style."

Davis played them two songs: "Flying Without Wings," which Clay liked, and "This Is the Night," which he loved. "I got chills. It was such an amazing song." To his delight, that was the song Clay and Josh would record if they made the top three. Kim and Ruben were designated to sing "Flying Without Wings." Aiken says Davis then "explained how they were going to be presented and how they were going to be orchestrated and arranged. It just excited us so much."

Once it got down to three finalists, Clay, Kim, and Ruben went in to record their respective singles. Aiken's overriding memory of that experience was that "Clive Davis is very particular, so we made a number of changes the next day and that was it."

To close the show, Ruben reprised "Flying Without Wings." While Ruben was singing, Clay made his way through the crowd to hug his mom, who was sitting with Ruben's mom, Emily, because the two women had become good friends. Before Clay left to go backstage, Emily grabbed him, kissed his cheek, and said proudly, "You did good, baby!"

After they met with the press, Clay and Ruben joined everyone at a party held at Sky Bar on the Sunset Strip; everyone, that is, except Ryan Seacrest, who begged off, claiming he was too sick. Some suspected he was a no-show because he had misread the voting figures not once but twice during the telecast and, apparently, had accidentally shown the results to Clay prior to the announcement.

The next morning Simon Cowell, who was suffering from a hangover, called a Los Angeles morning show to discuss the bungle. "Ryan is so brilliant, he had to see Clay and Ruben's names on a card, like he doesn't know who they are! What's amusing is Clay was trying to convince Ruben of this while Ryan was talking!"

The television station played a clip in slow motion that seemed to show Clay mouthing the words, "You won, I saw it!" Confused, Ruben asked, "I what?" After the clip, Simon complained that Clay had been "prattling like a schoolgirl through the whole thing!" However, despite having an excuse to twist the knife in Seacrest, Cowell was not upset.

Clay would later explain to the press that it wasn't like he was trying to sneak a peak. "We were backstage during the commercial right before the results were announced and we were all lining up getting ready to go out. Ryan had opened the card, just to kind of check. I glanced over and noticed that his card had a long name on it. So I made the assumption that it was him and not me because my name is kind of short. And so if you watch the tape back, I'm staring at Ruben the whole time."

One issue that wasn't so easily explained away was the inconsistent figures presented by Seacrest during the broadcast. Although he had alternately said there was a 1,300 then a 13,000 vote differential, the Fox network announced the following day the real differential was 134,000 and blamed the inaccuracies on a simple mistake. But conspiracy theorists refused to be so easily mollified. The issue was further inflamed by a rival network executive who gave an anonymous interview to the *Drudge Report*.

"Listen, I've been around Hollywood for a long, long time, and this reeks of a contrived, phony ending," the exec railed, adding that there should be an audit of Fox's results.

"Listen, we all get hurt when the viewer is misled, or tricked; I really think Fox, the show's producers, and even AT&T should open up the process, not hide behind secrecy or the complexity of counting so many votes over different time zones. Who or what told them this? A computer? Was there any human review? I know how this works, and I just do not think the truth is being told here."

An equally anonymous Fox exec shrugged off his rival's indignation. "As far as we are concerned, the votes are not in dispute. We are looking at how the bad math got on the air." Officially, Scott Grogin, vice president of corporate communications for Fox Broadcasting, told *Drudge,* "The host simply read incorrect information on a live broadcast." Furthermore Seacrest, it was revealed, had been sick and on medication the night of the finale.

Clay fans were quick to latch on to the suggestion of a conspiracy. Already, a group of fans had started an e-mail campaign requesting the FCC to investigate whether the competition had been fixed so that Ruben would win. A centerpiece of their suspicion was wide-ranging complaints from Clay fans that they had been unable to vote because the line was always busy. "My daughter dialed more than a hundred times and couldn't get through," Cynthia McGinnes of Chestertown, Maryland, complained to *USA Today.* "This is a show we all watch as a family, and I guarantee you we will never watch again. My daughter was in tears."

But a spokesperson from Verizon pointed out that the network was simply flooded because everybody was trying to dial in at the same time. The more technically savvy viewer turned to text messaging, and according to AT&T all of the messages got through. And as Fox's Grogin noted, "twenty-four million did get through. The system worked like it was supposed to."

On a more subjective front, fans also cried foul over what they perceived was Simon's efforts to promote Ruben by always complimenting him and never once suggesting he lose weight, the way he had several other finalists who were half Studdard's size.

Aiken tried to diffuse the controversy. "There was absolutely no rigging, absolutely no problem with the voting.

Everything was legit," he assured *TV Guide*. On *Larry King Live,* Aiken also refuted a story that ran in the *National Enquirer* which claimed Clay had e-mailed a Virginia man named Jason Drake saying the show was rigged. Clay expressed surprise and said he did not know anybody named Jason Drake. "That is a story that I haven't even heard yet. So I'm getting the breaking news from you," he told King. "But, no, it's absolutely not true. The producers on the show and the staff and Fox and all that stuff, there are standards and practices that are involved. It's a federal crime to rig a show. And we trust the producers so much. So there's absolutely no doubt in my mind that the show voting process is completely honest."

Clay admitted he was flattered that people cared so much but says the mistrust was misplaced. "I was on the show and involved closely in it for a long time, and I know everyone who was involved in it," he said during a *liveDaily* interview. "I totally trust the outcome of the show. I completely trust the results. Sometimes I just wish people would put their energies into supporting a charity or something like that instead of calling the FCC," he said, laughing.

But on a more serious note, Aiken worried how the ongoing argument might affect Studdard. "It concerns me because Ruben's a good, good friend of mine. I totally am proud of him and support everything that he does. Both of us really got exactly what we wanted out of this show. We both went into it hoping to get a recording contract and get this type of career and we both got it. He's got the title and that's what's different. Other than that, we're both having a great time and I'm totally happy with where I am. So, people who want to write letters can write letters to the Autism Society and help them out."

One thing about Clay, he would never ask more from others than he does from himself—which is why he was about to use his celebrity status to help others. He would combine his two passions and in the process help more people than he ever imagined possible.

Chapter Thirteen
Helping Others

It was still Clay's goal to graduate from college in December 2003, but with all of his touring, publicity, recording, and singing commitments, he and his professors needed to figure out a way for Clay to complete his necessary credits that wouldn't involve taking classes or student teaching.

The solution was to have Clay do an independent study project about nonprofits and special education. His specific assignment was to create a mock foundation that would work with kids with disabilities. Although some might question whether Clay was getting special treatment, most universities, including the University of North Carolina at Charlotte, permit independent study projects. Students are required to first submit a proposal, get permission from a supervising instructor to proceed, then have the proposal approved by a coordinator, the department chair, and the dean of the college.

"Independent studies actually have to be something which can be carried out without the regular contact that a course would have," Nancy Cooke explained in UNCC's *UT News*, saying she and Aiken kept in contact primarily through e-mail and phone calls. "This is similar to other independent study arrangements although, in many cases, the students are in the area, and can, if necessary, meet face to face more often with their instructors."

Clay's adviser, Wendy Wood, discussed his proposal with RealityTVWorld.com, saying, "Clay had a clear vision of what changes he would like to see with regard to services for, and acceptance of, individuals with developmental disabilities in schools and communities. But there was a great deal of work that he needed to do to determine if there was a niche for his idea for a foundation, to determine its mission, and to plan how the foundation would go about accomplishing its mission and objectives." In addition to conceptualizing the foundation, Aiken would also be responsible for doing an environmental study, and a business prospectus.

Clay began working on his project in late May 2003. He and Wood figured out when the project needed to be finished for him to be included in December graduation ceremonies. He was still working on it when the American Idol Tour began, and he would often mention the project to the performers and sometimes even to the audiences. The consistently positive responses he got made him realize that this could be so much more than just a project for school. This could be a way for him to continue helping kids *and* perform, a way to meld his two passions together for a cause he cared deeply about.

Initially, Clay's vision was modest, involving a foundation that would help kids back in his hometown and Charlotte. But by late June, he started to expand his dream. In its first week of release, Clay's single, "This Is the Night"/"Bridge Over Troubled Water," sold an astonishing 392,975 copies, outselling Studdard's "Flying Without Wings"/"Superstar" by about 107,000 copies. Then *Rolling Stone* featured Clay on the cover of its July 10 issue. This exposure further cemented Clay's popularity, which in turn could give the foundation the kick start it needed. "It began to look more and more like I really could create a foundation that helps kids with developmental disabilities not just in the Raleigh area but nationally and internationally," he'd say later. "American celebrities have an amazing amount of influence on the way America thinks, feels, and acts. I think that such an influence should be used in the most positive way possible."

Suddenly, Aiken caught a glimpse of what he felt was God's plan, and he firmly believed that through it all, there had been a divine hand guiding his life. During a visit to Buffalo, New York radio station Kiss 98.5, he described the process: "If I had not gone to school for special ed, if God had not put that in my path, I probably wouldn't be here today because I wouldn't have been working with the people who convinced me to audition for the show." And if not for the show, "I wouldn't be able to do the foundation, to hopefully make a difference in that area. There's so many things. Every day you look at where you are, and what you're doing. And you think, *God put me here for* this *reason. God made me meet* this *person for* this *reason. And God has* this *in store for me.* I just get excited about what's next and what he's got ready for me." That sense of being responsible to God's plan is why Clay works at being the best role model possible. "I would not be doing what he wanted me to do if I was not setting a good example for everybody who I speak with, everybody who I talk to, everybody who listens to me, or sees me on TV or [hears me on] the radio or even in person." And if Clay were going to move forward with a foundation, he knew there was one person he was supposed to make a part of it.

On Monday, July 28, 2003, Clay was in New York City to participate in the grand opening ceremonies for a new Wachovia Bank branch near Rockefeller Center. Also present was Mayor Michael Bloomberg. When he got the chance to speak, Aiken surprised everyone by announcing the formation of the Bubel/Aiken Foundation. He told the crowd, "The foundation is something I was going to have Wachovia help me set up and manage anyway, so I just thought, *Why not do it today?*

"Diane Bubel is a close friend of mine from home and she changed my life because she's the one who encouraged me to audition for *American Idol.* That's why I'm starting this foundation in her name. Hopefully we can make some positive changes in the lives of children with mental disabilities."

To help the foundation get off to a good start, Wachovia Bank presented Clay with a $10,000 donation, making Aiken's account the first official account at the Rockefeller Center branch.

The mandate of the foundation was to "provide grants and other one-on-one services to individuals living with disabilities so that they may participate in programs and work environments that are normally designed for persons without disabilities." The foundation would also "encourage and facilitate community inclusion and the empowerment of individuals with disabilities." Clay said his ultimate goal "is for this foundation to really make an impact. I hope this foundation has a much longer shelf life than I do."

Aiken described getting the foundation off the ground to *EP Magazine.* He said that everything started to take shape after he hired Chicago attorney Fran Skinner-Lewis to be the executive director. "Fran was so passionate about it, had the connections and knew what she was doing, so that's why it's become as big as it is. I continue to be involved. Fran does almost all of the footwork, but everything gets run by me. Any decision that's made is a joint decision." Together they assembled a group of special ed academics to develop a training curriculum, which the foundation uses to train YMCA employees in every state to work with children with disabilities.

Diane Bubel admitted in a *Spotlight Health* interview that when Clay told her what he was naming his foundation, she cried tears of appreciation and hope. Bubel believes the foundation can make a profound difference in the perception of children with mental disabilities.

"We want the message of the foundation to be inclusion—we want to 'open doors and open minds.' We want people to get to know our children and understand that by knowing them they will be better people. It's true in our family. My daughter Emma is more patient, wise, understanding and less self-indulgent than most kids her age because of Mike."

Aiken believes society as a whole will benefit from taking a more inclusive approach. "'Handicapped' is a label society puts on people. It's not something kids are born with. A child may have a disability but the handicap comes from society when they tell that child they can't do something. Our goal is to try and get rid of the barriers between individuals with disabilities and individuals without disabilities. And try to get people from all walks of life to be able to participate in programs together instead of just kids with disabilities having a camp and kids without disabilities having a camp. We want to get rid of the lines between them and integrate them and include them in everything together."

Besides giving kids self-esteem when they are treated like other students, Clay pointed out, "inclusion also helps kids academically and they start to pick up on socially correct behaviors. And the benefit is two-way. Kids without disabilities learn so much—possibly more. Instead of just seeing a kid with disabilities down the hall in a classroom, they get to learn about them. Ignorance leads to prejudice. Inclusion provides them an opportunity to learn compassion, acceptance, and tolerance—all skills which make our society better."

Something Oprah Winfrey had said—"It's not as much about being the American Idol as it is about what happens to you afterwards"—suddenly had special resonance for Clay. "As I became more involved in teaching, I saw children with developmental disabilities being turned away from inclusion in programs and so my dream became to fix this in some small way. There are so many kids and families that need our support. I am in a position now to be a voice for people with developmental disabilities. I think all of us have a higher purpose for what we are doing. The visible higher purpose for a celebrity is to create awareness for issues that need a voice. I'm just doing what I always planned on doing—teaching and helping children with developmental disabilities."

Not only did Clay want to show his appreciation to Diane for the part she had played in his pursuing *American Idol,* he knew she would be a vital, driving force behind the foundation because she had been an outspoken activist for years. When her son, Mike, was diagnosed with autism, she had to fight to get him the best education possible.

"There are programs for children with disabilities, but autism is a severe and profound disability and is often misunderstood," explained Diane. Although Mike remained nonverbal, at this point he was communicating by using picture cards and other objects. But Diane knows there are many children who haven't had the same opportunities as her son. "The foundation has given me a new focus and the opportunity to do something really good for those who deserve to be understood. I will continue to make a difference in my son's life and hope to impact the lives of other individuals with the same challenges."

In *Clay Aiken Unplugged,* his professors at UNCC reacted with amazement and pride at what Clay was able to accomplish. "He was given gifts in special education with his passion for students with disabilities but also singing and the world of fame," observed Cheryl Young. She added it was amazing "that he's taken his Bubel/Aiken Foundation and combined his fame with children with disabilities."

Nancy Cooke, who worked with Clay on his project, was excited by the opportunity Clay had to make a difference. "I'm extremely proud of Clay, but what I'm really excited about is that he is just such a wonderful advocate. And it's those values that he's maintained. Many people would be drawn away from that focus. He's been able to maintain it. And it's great for us how he has been able to shine a light on the special education program here at the university, which is wonderful, but he is an ambassador for special needs children and adults. I'm so delighted with the Bubel/Aiken Foundation, his work on it, and his ambition to do it."

Although the project enabled Clay to meet the requirements for graduating, he still would not be able to get a teaching license until he completed student teaching.

"Most people finishing their degree are also finishing student teaching and are also applying for their license," noted Cooke, who added somewhat wistfully, "Maybe some day he will, and I know he's going to be wonderful teaching."

Unlike many advocates who struggle in obscurity, Aiken's celebrity would open more doors more quickly, noted Fred Spooner. "He had the opportunity to go to Washington and meet with several folks on Capitol Hill who very much support issues in the area of people with disabilities. I've been on Capitol Hill several times on business, but when I go I get to meet with the twenty-some-year-old assistant; Clay got to meet with Senator Tom Harkin and his people from Iowa; he met with Ted Kennedy."

While Clay was earning the reputation as both a successful recording artist and advocate for people with disabilities, Ruben was getting publicity of the negative kind. On July 20, 2003, the same day Aiken was in Washington, D.C., to promote a film education program and to sing "Happy Birthday" to Senator Elizabeth Dole, Studdard was in the news for having filed a lawsuit against clothing maker 205 Flava, which had supplied Ruben with all his now-trademark 205 jerseys. Studdard was asking for a share of the profits from an estimated $2 million in sales Flava earned thanks to Ruben's having worn the jerseys on the show.

The filing claimed, "Without capitalizing on and exploiting Studdard's huge popularity, defendants would not have the sales and name recognition that they are currently enjoying throughout the nation and outside the United States." Part of the issue was also that 205 Flava had published pictures of the singer from *American Idol* without his permission. Studdard's business adviser told reporters, "I want Ruben to be rewarded for his success via merchandise sales. I don't want people to prosper if they are exploiting my friend."

The owners of 205 Flava, Fred and Willie Jenkins, begged to disagree, expressing bewilderment at the action since from the beginning the company had "been behind him 110 percent." But the Jenkins brothers came back fighting against the claim that Ruben had not been compensated. On Monday, August 3, the attorney for Fred and Willie Jenkins, LaVeeda Morgan Battle, held a news conference and dropped a bombshell.

Not only had they paid Studdard, but he had been getting paid while he was still competing on the show—a clear violation of Fox Broadcasting rules that strictly prohibited *American Idol* contestants from entering into outside contracts while on the show. To back up his assertion, the lawyer showed reporters canceled checks totaling $10,000 made out to Ruben's brother Kevin and his manager Ron Edwards. It was also asserted that Ruben was initially paid $1,000 a week to wear the company's clothes, but the longer he stayed on the show, the more money he wanted. Furthermore, said Battle, Ruben obviously knew that what he was doing broke the rules, because he asked the company to keep the payments a secret.

Michael Jaffa, vice president of business and legal affairs for American Idol Productions, Inc., explained why such an arrangement is problematic for the network and producers. "We have major sponsors like Old Navy. There are issues promoting a brand in competition with our sponsors."

After learning of the allegations, one network official confirmed that if the deal had come out while the show was still going on, Studdard would have been immediately disqualified from the competition. The incident led the network and producers to take extra precautions against such deals ever happening in the future. However, this wasn't the Olympics, and all concerned took the attitude that what was done was done. Nobody would be asking Ruben to symbolically give up his American Idol crown.

But in the eyes of many Ruben fans, their idol never got the chance to really enjoy his win, because it seemed as if in the end, Clay was the more sought after of the two. It was

Aiken, not Studdard, to make it on the cover of *Rolling Stone* first. There were the charges of voting irregularities and of judge favoritism. Even though on its own merit, Ruben's single "Flying Without Wings" was a smash success—it sold over 280,000 copies in its first week when the average is 5,000—Clay's single was an even greater success. Then came the news that, because of unexpected production delays, Clay's album would be released a full month before Ruben's.

Then there was the fan reaction on the American Idol Tour. While all the finalists received warm receptions, it was impossible not to hear that Clay was emerging as the audience favorite. An online article by W. Scott Pavone offered review snippets to emphasize Clay's growing stature.

> "Aiken . . . showed true star quality. Not only was he a natural onstage, conversing with confidence and glee, but he also commanded the stage." *(Minneapolis Star-Tribune)*
>
> "When Clay started into his hit single, 'This Is the Night,' the screaming was so loud it drowned out most of his vocals. When he appeared onstage later in the evening wearing a Minnesota Wild hockey shirt—well, our ears are still ringing. . . . Clay was the crowd's clear favorite." *(Pioneer Press)*
>
> "Kimberley Locke finally introduced *Rolling Stone* cover boy Clay Aiken, whipping the crowd into an ear-bloodying frenzy of Nickelodeon-sculpted screams." *(Chicago Sun-Times)*
>
> "If there was a winner of this perpetual competition, it was Aiken. While he and Studdard have comparably strong voices . . . only Aiken has the natural charm to do justice to the 'Idol' mantle. Expect him to steal your heart. . . . [T]he evening was all about Aiken and Studdard. When the former appeared on stage, the volume from his screaming fans nearly overwhelmed his voice." *(Chicago Tribune)*

> "Move over Ruben, it's now Clay's show." *(Toronto Sun)*

> "One thing was clear after seeing these kids play live. While Ruben Studdard was likely voted American Idol fair and square, the people's Idol is, without a doubt, Clay Aiken." (chartattack.com)

Part of the discrepancy probably had to do with their disparate personalities. Studdard is a laid-back man who often comes across as shy. Aiken, on the other hand, loves to talk and is quick with a quip or snappy sound bite. He is also relentlessly polite and charming, which, combined with his vocal talent, makes him ready-made for mass media. "I honestly think Clay Aiken has changed this competition forever," Simon Cowell observed, "because I think it's becoming incredibly personality-led now, inevitably."

Paula Abdul wondered aloud whether Ruben felt cheated out of his moment in the spotlight. "I often wonder what's going through Ruben's head and his heart. I think a lot of people have expressed that he doesn't get to feel like he won because of Clay."

Among those who allegedly felt Aiken was stealing Ruben's rightful thunder were members of Ruben's family. *In Touch Weekly* reported that Ruben's uncle Brian Studdard labeled Clay "a bad loser. He had pink and white furniture in his room. He's not the sort of guy you'd choose to be an American Idol." According to the article, Ruben's aunt, Sylvia Studdard, added, "I don't care if he's outselling Ruben in the charts. People should just accept it. He didn't win and he's *not* the American Idol—Ruben is."

Both Clay and Ruben went to great lengths to downplay any notion of ill feelings or rivalry, with Aiken bluntly saying he refused to be drawn into any controversy. "It's definitely not a rivalry at all. It's more of a competition with *myself* and I think Ruben feels the same way. It's just about me doing the best that I can do and I know that for him it's about him doing the best that he can do," Aiken told AP Radio. "I support him. I would be the first person in line to get his album—and he better be the first person in line to get mine!

"*American Idol* wasn't a competition between who was better, necessarily, it was just a competition between what America preferred," Clay continued. "So when the albums come out, do people prefer to have a CD of what he sings or what I sing? That's all it's about." Clay believed there was plenty of room for both of them to be successful.

When pressed about whether Ruben ever seemed resentful of all the attention Clay had been getting, Aiken replied, "He seems to be fine with it."

And indeed, there were no signs of turmoil reported during the summer 2003 tour with Clay, Studdard, and the other finalists. According to Clay, being on the road as a group was an unforgettable adventure. "It's extremely flattering every single night. Every night something's different and new. Last night I had panties thrown on the stage," he revealed during a phone interview with *liveDaily*. "It's all a new experience. It's something that we all wanted to do for so long. We're just enjoying the ride and trying to take it all in."

Despite the close quarters, all the performers were relaxed and enjoying themselves. "We know each other so well," Clay said. "I think that's what's so cool about it. We've all known each other for nine months now. We know where everybody came from. We're all just friends. Nobody gets starstruck at anybody. Everybody's just hangin'. We've known each other for so long that we're really like a family. We definitely enjoy being together and we really perform well together. We used to rehearse for the show and just have the nastiest rehearsals on Wednesday mornings and Wednesday afternoons. Then when the show hit the airwaves on Wednesday nights, our medleys would come together flawlessly. That's just the way the whole show has worked because we know each other so well."

From Second Place to the Top of the Charts

When the tour ended in August 2003, Clay decided that it was time to start weaning himself away from his tightly woven connection with *American Idol* in order to start forging his own musical identity. And as it turned out, the first step away from the nest would be with Miss Independence herself.

Chapter Fourteen
Life After Idol

Within days after the *American Idol 2* finale, Clay had his first meeting with record executives about his album. Aiken told Reuters that while he and Ruben were in New York doing a press tour, "I had a meeting with Clive Davis at his house in Connecticut, where he and Tom Ennis from 19 Entertainment, Steve Ferrera and I went up and listened to the stuff they already had prepared for me." To Clay's surprise, they had begun selecting songs "even before the second season was over."

But that was exactly one of Davis's duties—matching songs, songwriters, and producers to recording artists. Davis, who discovered many hit singers, including Whitney Houston, told Clay that life after *American Idol* would present many challenges. "I told him that he is a marvelous talent and that 'This Is the Night' is a very strong song, but it is a souvenir of a television show, and we have to get beyond that," the executive recounted to *Time*. "It is my feeling that when you get into being a career recording artist, the stakes are different. People want to see if you can stretch and evolve. They want to know if you have some edge."

Aiken, politely but firmly, reminded the legendary music mogul that his success was not based on edge; it was based on the people—and families—who tuned in every week to watch *American Idol,* and that's who he wanted to make the album for. Beyond that, it would go against Clay's deep-seated personal beliefs to stray too far from who he was; in other words, no sex or even suggestive lyrics.

"Clive tried to tell me that saying certain words in a song—or as he says, 'putting some balls into it'—isn't bad, it's just strong emotion," Aiken recalled in a *Time* profile. "Well, there are certain words and emotions I don't want kids hearing, and I'm not changing because they think it's going to sell better. This is going to sound horrible, but I got 12 million votes doing what I did."

Aiken really meant it when he told writer Carla Hay, "The most important responsibility a celebrity has is to set an example and be a role model. I want to make sure that no matter how long I go through this, I don't fall into the trap of changing and modifying how I do things that aren't a positive example. I want to remain somebody that the entire family can listen to or watch."

Clive Davis got to the top of the music business by staying ahead of the curve and tailoring his artists' music for radio play and MTV consumption. It didn't seem as if Clay would have the final word on anything. But a funny thing had happened to the music business over the previous five years: it had been brought to its knees by file sharing and angry consumers. While industry executives wanted to lay the blame for its trouble solely at the feet of those who used Napster, Morpheus, or Kazaa, some analysts suggested the labels should shoulder just as much, if not more, of the blame. Rampant greed seemed to be the focus of that argument. Where labels talked of protecting their financial interest in copyrighted material, consumers accused the industry of not giving record buyers what they wanted because labels had been loath to give up their monopolistic control of how music is marketed and enjoyed. Even when the industry had acquiesced and offered music online, the costs were out of line with the price of overhead. People wondered, *How is it they can justify charging ninety-nine cents for a download—music for which they did not have to package or ship or inventory—when if broken down that's the same prorated cost of the song on a CD bought at a music store?*

With attitudes toward labels and their executives at an all-time low, suddenly the industry needed Aiken, and more importantly his fan base. According to research, the *American*

Idol audience buying Clay's records were not Napster users. Interestingly, they would not even be classified as avid music fans or regular music buyers, meaning it was Clay bringing them to the checkout lines.

According to sales records, an unusually high percentage of "This Is the Night" singles were bought at Wal-Mart and Target stores. This was no accident. RCA had intentionally rented the space to reach consumers who don't normally browse the music section. Gerry Lopez, who runs Handleman Entertainment Resources, the company that stocks music at stores, observed in *Time,* "Our consumer is the middle 80 percent of the population. . . . We're not catering to Napster or Kazaa folks, just people who like a nice song sung by a nice kid."

Of course, for many executives in the music business in general and at RCA in particular, this trend signaled the end of the music world as they knew it. It galled many employees that the label that is synonymous with Elvis, the King of Rock and Roll, had become the American record distributor for someone who in their eyes was a bland talent contest *loser.* Simon Fuller and his team at 19 Entertainment, the official record label of the series, shrugged off this whining as so much sour grapes.

"Simon Fuller did not create *American Idol* to be in the television business," Tom Ennis from 19 Entertainment reminded *Time.* "He created *American Idol* as a new way to find talent, to manage and nurture it." Because Fuller created the series, he had as much say-so as Clive Davis or anyone else at RCA in how the album for any *Idol* finalist turned out. And Fuller wanted the *Idol* audience to be served first and foremost. "You can't skew yourself one way and not speak to the people who spent all that time watching you and voting for you," Ennis said.

So the question became, how should the label sell Clay if not as budding sex symbol or female fantasy? The songs they ultimately picked were intended to show off Clay's biggest asset—his voice. Aaron Borns, RCA's senior director of marketing, said, "People want to take potshots at him because he was discovered on television, so you have to remind people how great a singer he is. That's what's going to carry him through beyond the misconception that he's a one-hit wonder."

Even though executives had started the process without him, Aiken claims there was collaboration once he joined the party. "I went into it pretty apprehensively, not knowing what to expect. I had been told by a number of people that if you get half of what you want on your first album, you're doing really well. Pretty much every single thing they had was something that I liked." He told Reuters that Davis "played nine to ten songs and none of them really put me out of my comfort zone. They were all things that I thought were radio-friendly, and I was really happy. So the very first conversation I had in the business was a big surprise to me, because I was not really prepared for being as happy as I was." In the end, Clay said, "There were maybe one or two songs I didn't like, and they were taken off the album quickly." Clay would also have the first music video shot for "This Is the Night" scrapped because he felt it tried to portray him in a way "that's just not me."

Because the label and Fuller wanted to take advantage of Clay's *Idol* popularity, Clay had recorded much of the album prior to the American Idol Tour in July. RCA Records general manager Richard Sanders said it was up to the label to capitalize on all the exposure Clay had been given on the series. "The first thing that you have to recognize is the power of TV and the vast audience it does have. A vehicle that week in and week out generates millions of viewers to see your artist is the most powerful marketing tool you can have right now. It's not a question of if you win or lose; it's a question of how you relate to the audience that's watching you each week.

"In the environment we're in now, it's difficult to have a mainstream pop artist, especially a solo male artist, be launched in a credible manner without any rhythmic urban base. We knew we had the audience for Clay. So the task was to find the best material."

Whether or not Sanders agreed with the direction Clay wanted to go, or didn't want to go, with his image, and whether or not he agreed that *American Idol* could be bad for music creativity in the long haul, he wouldn't say. All he would say to *Time* was that he was "a disciple of the phenomenon. There is no *Ed Sullivan Show* anymore, no opportunity for two or three generations to listen to music together and have a good time. I'm into being the guy that provides that.

"I've told everyone . . . Americans buy more vanilla ice cream than any other flavor. Yes, they like their Rocky Road and Cherry Garcia, but ultimately America wants to consume vanilla. So we're going to sell the best vanilla. Given the problems we're facing as an industry, we cannot afford to be judgmental."

Picking up on that analogy, Aiken later told writer Rick Massimo, "People call me, all the time, vanilla, which I don't find insulting at all. It's the most popular flavor; you can't make half the flavors without vanilla. I think that critics find that to be less credible, but the public seems to be happy with it, and I'm happy to fill that opportunity."

When asked by a *Minneapolis Star-Tribune* writer if he was insulted when *Time* magazine quoted an RCA executive calling Aiken a Barry Manilow with less talent, Clay retorted, "Barry Manilow is still around, isn't he? So I don't mind it. There are certain people who aren't still around. There are people from the eighties and the early nineties who did what would get them successful for one minute and didn't consider thirty years down the road. Barry Manilow has been around a long time. Rod Stewart has been around a long time. Norah Jones will be around for a long time, because she's not necessarily interested in making a quick fast buck; she's interested in giving people what they want."

It was Aiken's belief that even though no record label, including RCA, would have let him or Ruben in the door, both he and Studdard had hit singles and record contracts because that's what the American public as a whole wanted to hear. They didn't want just the twenty songs radio stations played on rotation, the same ones that were being heavily promoted by the record companies.

Despite all the philosophical disagreements, there was still an album to be made, and in the end, it would be made Clay's way as far as tone and having G-rated, family-friendly content. Aiken began working on *Measure of a Man* shortly after the *Idol* finale. Because Davis hooked him up with a variety of songwriters and producers, Clay ended up recording in several cities. "They put me right into the studio in Los Angeles. I spent about four weeks recording pretty heavily in L.A. and Miami and then I flew to London to record there."

Despite working in some of the most exciting cities in the world, Aiken did not do much sightseeing or exploring. In Miami, he recorded "Invisible" at Desmond Child's studio. "I'm not a big sun lover. I burn, so Miami was spent inside the studio, in the dark studio," he admitted to *Billboard*. "Ruben was very upset with me. He said I should have gone out. And then in complete contrast, we finished it up and added a few quick changes in Minneapolis. So we went from sunny Miami to cold and windy Minneapolis."

In London, Aiken recorded "Touch." He told Nick Rogers of the Springfield, Illinois *State Journal-Register* that the best part of the trip for him was flying Virgin Atlantic. "This is the best airline on the planet when you're flying overseas because you get a massage on the plane. So it was great."

Less great was trying to navigate in a different country. "I would get to the hotel and everything would be closed and I would not know my way around, would not know how to use the ATM machine because what's this funny-looking money it's handing me out? I asked for twenty dollars. Who is this woman on the money?" He told Fred Bronson that when he got to his hotel, there was construction going on nearby, making it impossible to sleep. He also complained that maids would come in and wake him up, asking if he needed his bed made. So it was a sleep-deprived singer who arrived to work with producer Dave Erickson. "I was so dead tired, I slept in the studio. I recorded one verse, came out just to sit down for a second, ended up falling asleep and an hour later, I woke up and he had let me sleep the entire time, which I thought was so nice."

Clay had been forewarned that London would probably be damp, foggy, and misty. Instead, he said, "It was sunny the entire time we were there. I just didn't get a chance to experience anything. I asked the cab driver to drive me past Buckingham Palace so that I could see it."

Overall, Aiken says recording the first album was a great learning experience. "I went into it open-minded, knowing that I didn't know much and that I should be prepared to learn stuff," he said in the *Time* profile. "I really wasn't surprised by much except how often Clive Davis sent me back into the studio to record over. As a producer, he is meticulous."

Although some singers resist working with so many producers on one project, Clay felt it was beneficial for him, telling *Billboard,* "I think that was the nicest part about recording this album, because I did work with so many different producers that I was able to get an idea of how I want to do this when I go into the studio next time."

It's somewhat ironic that for as much as Clay loves big ballads, he feels little empathy with most of the songs. Songs that deal with love lost or the pain of rejection do not have personal resonance with him. For example, he says the album cut "No More Sad Songs" is "probably the hardest to identify with, because it's very angst-ridden. It's got a lot of *You wronged me* and *I'm getting rid of you* and *I'm happy* and *I'm going to go on with my life and forget you*—and I've not done that. It's a little difficult for me to identify with right now. Hopefully I won't have to identify with it; I don't think that's a bad thing that you've never been hurt that bad. So singing these songs where I really haven't been in that situation, I've had to act. So it is a lot about acting."

Although it was originally planned that Ruben's album would debut first, production delays and creative disagreements pushed back Studdard's release date well into November 2003. Since Aiken's record was ready to go, the decision was made to release it October 14, 2003, a change of schedule Clay says Ruben approved of. "He is nothing if not a friend and a true gentleman."

While promoting the album, Clay assured fans he had stayed true to his musical and personal beliefs. "I still think we did exactly what I set out to do: make good music without offending anybody. Make something everybody could listen to in the car without having to turn it down for children." That said, he did allow that "there's definitely been a progression" artistically. "These songs are a little edgier. We've made them more radio friendly. They're definitely more modern types of songs than I sang on the show."

In a Reuters news service interview, Aiken said he was pleased about how well the album turned out. "The nice thing about it is that it's not a huge departure for me. The record company, myself, and the management group have been able to really agree on what we'd like to see from it. We're not going to see a lot of hard-core, inappropriate stuff that I'm not all for. A lot of the stuff is like 'This Is the Night.' It's a pop-flavored album. I think there's a lot of people out there who may not be the best influence for kids. I wouldn't want my kids listening to some of the stuff out there. None of the stuff on the album is like that."

When asked if he would follow Ruben's lead and perhaps start writing his own songs, Aiken admitted the thought had crossed his mind, but for him, it was all about what was best for the record. "There are artists who I won't name, who write songs because it's a way to make some more money on their album. On those albums, usually the first three songs are written by someone else, and they're great, and the rest of the album that the artist writes is mediocre. They make a little more money, but then the album won't sell as well. So if money is the motivation, it's the wrong motivation. That said, I don't think I have the talent and I don't really have anything to say. So if I wrote music at this point, the motivation would be the money, and I won't do that."

It was interesting to hear that Aiken was finding it difficult to get excited about the album's pending release. "It's hard to step back from all of this and look at it as an outsider looking in," he admitted to Reuters. "Maybe when I get it in my hand, I'll get excited about it."

With all the changes in his life over the preceding year, it's understandable if Clay was a bit numb. He had settled in Los Angeles, sharing a house with fellow finalist Kim Locke. When reporter Nick Rogers asked what Locke's worst habit was, Aiken sidestepped the question.

"It's not a bad habit, I guess. She gets up early. She's an early riser, and I'm not such an early riser. She gets up in the morning and makes breakfast. And it's not that she's loud, but it's that it smells so good and it wakes me up. But she does it in her underwear sometimes, which I guess is probably not the best idea."

Aiken then tattled on himself, admitting he was "pretty messy. She keeps her room as dirty as possibly can be, but the rest of the house she keeps very clean. Me, on the other hand, my room is not so bad, but the rest of the stuff—like the living room and everything—I just leave stuff lying around all the time."

The best part about rooming with Locke, Clay told PBS Kids, is that they share similar values and "have the same outlook on life. We're both enjoying this for what it is and we're both realistic and realize it may last for a long time or may last for a year, so we're just going to enjoy and have fun with it."

He also talked about always having close female friends. "You don't have to be either dating or not friends. There can be a middle ground and that's what a platonic relationship is. I think platonic relationships can be closer than dating relationships sometimes—dating relationships end and platonic relationships are going to be there no matter what."

Family would also always be there. Aiken has kept in close contact with his mom and was thrilled the day he was able to pay off the mortgage on her house, letting her own it free and clear. But, careful with his finances, he did very little splurging other than to buy himself a Volvo to drive in L.A. and a second car to keep back in Raleigh for when he visited there.

Not that money was going to be an issue for long. Those at RCA who worried that Aiken's appeal would not last past the television show were quickly quieted when sales figures were reported. In its first week of release, *Measure of a Man* sold a stunning 613,000 copies. It was official—Clay was a bona fide star.

Clay learned quickly to read album reviews at his own peril because many dismissed both his music and his sudden rise to fame, claiming it wasn't the music that was appealing but the prepackaged marketing, akin to what sells cereal or soft drinks, that drove sales. "I don't read reviews," he confirmed to Carla Hay. "I don't think it matters what reviewers think. I think that's just one person's opinion, so bad reviews don't really matter to me." And as he pointedly noted, "The sales of *Measure of a Man* have definitely contradicted those bad reviews."

Not only did the album sales vindicate Aiken, so did the awards that started coming his way. In November 2003, Clay won the Fan's Choice Award at the American Music Awards. When accepting his trophy, Clay joked, "I'm not used to winning anything. I'm kind of used to second place." Then a month later, he won the *Billboard* Award for Best-selling Single of the Year for "This Is the Night"/"Bridge Over Troubled Water."

For all Clay's initial success, though, *Idol* judge Randy Jackson put it in perspective. "I think the albums are okay but the success of the first album by any of the winners or runners-up is really more about the success of the show," he said. "I think it's going to be the second album that's going to determine if they really, really have it."

Aiken feels that the path to long-term success has to be traveled slowly and carefully and has to lead away from *American Idol.* He tried to explain the balance he was looking for to Carla Hay. "I am very grateful for *American Idol,* obviously, but it is a double-edged sword. On one hand, I can never discount the fact that if it weren't for the show this wouldn't be happening. But the show has also held a few of us back a little. I long for the day when the fact that I was on *American Idol* becomes a side note. The reason people come to my shows and buy my album is because I can sing. I don't want the show to define who I am."

Clay also admitted he didn't want to be permanently known as a runner-up all his professional life. "I'd love to be able to establish myself on my own and not always be the contestant. A lot of people feel *American Idol* contestants are game-show participants and are not real artists. That's a stigma we'd all love to get rid of."

To that end, Clay's next move in January 2004 was to announce he would be going out on tour with Kelly Clarkson. To some, this seemed an odd choice for two people who were desperately trying to lose the *American Idol* label, but to Aiken, it was a logical first step in branching out on his own.

While visiting radio station Z100, Clay explained that originally, he and Clarkson had each planned a solo tour. "Kelly had a tour and I had a tour. And then we just decided at the last minute to throw them together and do them together. That's why we called it the Independent Tour." Combining the two acts allowed the performers to play bigger venues and "have someone on the road to kind of share the load with and to have fun with." The hope was to show fans that while both performers hailed from *American Idol,* both had evolved and matured into performers who should be recognized on their own merits.

The Independent Tour was a financial success and allowed Clay to get more experience performing on the road. By spring 2004, he was ready to take the next step and go out on his own.

Chapter Fifteen
The Glass Has Water

For all the success Clay Aiken achieved in 2003, one of his proudest days came in December when he graduated from the University of North Carolina at Charlotte with his degree in special education. Unfortunately, the commencement wasn't without some controversy and a smattering of ill will. First, some students were upset that each graduate would be limited to seven tickets, a stipulation made in an effort to prevent Aiken fans and other gawkers to attend and potentially disrupt the ceremony. A petition was circulated that requested the ceremony be moved to a larger venue, which the administration declined.

The students with relatives who had already made travel arrangements felt it was unfair that their families should be denied attendance just because Aiken was present. This animosity in turn caused some students to openly question whether Clay was even eligible to graduate—as far as they knew, he'd been off being a singing star for the past year. To answer the criticism and silence the rumors, Clay permitted the college to publicly discuss what would otherwise have been confidential school records. The records clearly showed Aiken had, thanks to the independent study project, successfully completed all the requirements to graduate. As it turned out, the administration granted extra tickets at the last minute, and according to the Associated Press, the arena ended up being only two-thirds full.

At the commencement, Clay was the last graduate to receive his diploma because Chancellor James Woodward had asked him to address the class. Clay couldn't help hearing a chorus of boos interspersed with the applause. But he maintained his composure and said, "This has been an amazing year for me. This is more special to me than a lot of the things that have happened to me this year, because what happens here today says something to people. This is a day that makes for all of us a statement, how important it is to persevere and continue to work and strive to succeed. Thank you for letting me be a part of this day. Congratulations and God bless. Thank you so much."

Afterward, some UNCC students vented their anger on the NinerOnline Web site. According to the *Collegiate Standard,* one graduate wrote: "The whole thing was a big charade and I felt like an uninvited guest at my own graduation. There I was, scrambling for my last couple of hours to get my degree, while UNCC had pretty much already decided to give Clay his degree back in November when they sprung this crap on all of us . . . no questions asked. And I'm supposed to feel sorry for Clay because he was mildly booed? . . . Yeah right."

Later, the *Charlotte Observer* published an article written by Clay saying how thankful he was to have participated in the commencement, that it was "every bit as exciting and memorable" as being selected for *American Idol* and performing in the Macy's Thanksgiving Day Parade, and that he wouldn't have missed the experience "for anything in the world." The letter went on to say, in part:

> While I truly regret any inconvenience my attendance may have caused, I am grateful to have had the chance to come back to UNC Charlotte to celebrate this milestone. A triumph four years in the making, this was a "magical moment" that I wanted to capture—for myself and those whose support made it possible.
>
> In what could be the understatement of the year, my life has changed dramatically since that first *American Idol* tryout. Yet fame and glory are fleeting, especially in the music business. That's

> why completing my degree and graduating from college were priorities. How long this ride will last is anyone's guess, but the fact remains that if it all ended tomorrow, I'd still have Plan A to fall back on—and that's not a typo. My first dream was to work with children with disabilities. . . .
>
> If my career detour from special education to singing has done one thing, it has afforded me the opportunity to make a difference in the lives of others. In founding the Bubel/Aiken Foundation, we hope to be able to help families receive much-needed support with the care and education of their special needs children. . . .
>
> Thomas Wolfe said you can't go home again, and now I understand. In 12 months, my life has changed forever. . . . I missed out on some opportunities due to schedule conflicts—and while those windows may open again, second chances aren't guaranteed. I did not want my college commencement to fall into that category. . . .
>
> I hope that my participation in UNC Charlotte's commencement sends a clear signal that far outlasts whatever fame my future holds: there is nothing more important than obtaining an education.

Later, during an interview with the *Seattle Post-Intelligencer,* Aiken admitted the situation during graduation had been awkward. "I don't know how thrilled they were to have me at the graduation. The school was excited about it, but the students were not. It was a little bit of a buzz-kill for them to have so much attention around me every day and not around them."

Not one to dwell or be filled with angst, Aiken chose to tuck away the good memories of the day and move forward. So it was only two weeks after the Independent Tour with

Kelly Clarkson wrapped that Clay announced he would embark on a solo tour. It would run from July 6 and last at least three months. The venues, primarily in cities east of the Mississippi, ranged from two engagements at Caesar's Palace in Atlantic City to county and state fairs, again reflecting the wide cross section of fans Aiken has had.

Clay spoke of his fans in glowing terms to *Fox All Access*. "I'm constantly amazed by how enthusiastic they are. They know things before I know it sometimes. They honestly do. I find out things about where I'm going to be from the fans. My mom will call me and say, 'I read on the Internet you're going to be doing Nickelodeon this Saturday.' 'Huh? Well, let me call and check. . . .' and lo and behold, 'Oh, yeah, we were going to tell you. . . .'

"They are also very protective. They are always concerned whether I'm getting enough sleep or getting enough to eat." Aiken joked that his fans had become equally as concerned about his security man, Jerome. "He gets sent flowers and gets cards saying, 'Thanks for taking care of Clay.' They are very energetic and protective and extremely dedicated. I don't know what I did to deserve them."

Because of the number of fans who write him, though, his whole family has become involved in going through his mail and organizing the letters. "It's become work for everybody," he said, mostly because he doesn't want some paid-for service answering fan mail. "There are seventeen boxes of fan mail at the house and when I go home, we go through it because we open every one of them."

Clay has worried that all the attention he gets might somehow be a burden to his younger brother. "I said to Brett the other day, 'I know you're sick of me. I'd be sick of me.' But Brett's been so patient with it all. He's been so good with it all. I don't know if I could have done it. I feel sad sometimes for Brett and for Jeff because more than anything, I do not ever want them to lose their identity and become 'Clay Aiken's brother.'"

Clay is particularly mindful to make time for young fans with disabilities. While performing in Atlanta in December 2003, a teenage girl with cerebral palsy was brought backstage to meet him. The girl's father told Net Music Countdown that Aiken treated her like a princess. "Even though Jennifer can be difficult to understand when she speaks, Clay listened intently and understood everything she told him. He must have spent ten or fifteen minutes with her. This was her one wish in life. I hope Clay knows how much he helped her."

While Clay seems genuinely to enjoy and appreciate his fans, he has more mixed feelings about fame. It astonishes him how every move he makes is under someone's watchful eye. He gave an example in a *Billboard* interview. "I was in Raleigh for a day or two really quickly in June, and a friend of mine, Amanda, picked me up at the airport. We went by my old high school, to see some of the teachers I hadn't seen since high school. Within an hour, not only was it on the Internet that Amanda and I were driving around I-540 in Raleigh in her black Jetta, but there were pictures of us at the school posted on the Internet. That's how fast things get around."

On one level, Clay said the scrutiny doesn't bother him because he's not ever doing anything he'd worry about people knowing. "As long as you're living right, then you don't have to worry about what people see." On the other hand, he does worry about being put on too high a pedestal. He said the biggest misconception would be to view him as some kind of angel or perfect boy next door. "I have a temper," he said. "I make rash judgments. I yell at people. I am not perfect."

But being in the constant spotlight has made him feel as if he has to try to be perfect all the time, "and I'm not," he assured Fred Bronson. "That's been somewhat complicated for me, because I want to make sure that I'm being genuine and being friendly to everybody, because it's not like me to be rude and ignore somebody. If I'm eating dinner, and you come up and say hello, that's fine."

A bigger issue has been that Clay finds it difficult to go out and do everyday things. While in Indiana on tour, he recounted an experience to the *South Bend Tribune.* "Yesterday I went to the mall for the first time in a number of months. I wanted to hang out, so I put my hat on and tried to walk around the mall as discreetly as possible.

"We were only there about an hour before we started getting noticed and chased and followed around and stopped. And that's kind of difficult. I didn't nearly get to do anything. I bought a pillow from Sears. I would have loved to have gone into the record store and seen what was for sale and what was out, but I can't go into those anymore because my picture is up everywhere.

"This time last year, I could have walked to the grocery store, or walked my dog out on my neighborhood street and not had a problem with it. Now, my dog only gets to go pee in the backyard because I can't go out in the front yard because people actually drive by my house because they think I'm home."

However, there have been some definite perks to being so recognizable, he admitted to *Teen People.* "I went to the DMV in Raleigh and they let me cut straight to the front of the line! There are definitely upsides, but the downside is no anonymity anymore. "

Through it all, though, Aiken tries to keep his sense of humor. "I have my own personal member of the paparazzi now. He meets me at the airport and follows me around. His name is Sam. He wasn't there when I walked out of the studio today, and I said, 'Where is Sam?' I was genuinely concerned."

Whenever he starts to feel fed up, Clay reminds himself there are 69,999 other people who would gladly trade places with him. "Somebody once said, 'You asked for it,'" he mused in an *Ability* magazine interview. "And I thought, 'Did I really ask for it?'"

When asked if the glass was half empty, Clay laughed and quipped, "The glass has water in it; that's all I know."

"I know he's grounded, so I'm not worried about people changing him," Clay's mother is quoted in *EP Magazine.* "I'm not worried that he will become like some celebrities who feel like they have to say yes to everything. I think if he has to change himself, he'd just get out of the business." But she said she is concerned "that he might become a recluse and not go anywhere. I worry that he won't have a life of his own."

Perhaps the most perplexing consequence of being in the public eye has been the ongoing speculation about Clay's sexuality. During an interview with Diane Sawyer he implied that he's a virgin; he is known for his close friendships with women, none of which are romantically inclined; no former girlfriend has come forward to talk about what it was like to date him; and his professed best friend is a young man who toured with Clay but nobody in the press has met or interviewed, the way they have, say Amy, Amanda, or Angela.

Aiken has shrugged it off. "One thing I've found of people in the public eye is either you're a womanizer or you've got to be gay. Since I'm neither one of those, people are completely concerned about me. They're like, 'What are you, then?' I'm sure it has to do with being raised by women. I wouldn't want somebody gawking at my mom and grabbing her butt and catcalling at her, trying to hook up with her at a bar. I'm not saying I'm not going to look. Hello! But you know what I mean?"

Clay recalled to *Cosmo Girl,* "Ruben used to say to me, 'Look at all these panties they're throwing you onstage. You could get any girl in this room!' But I'm not interested in getting any girl in the room—I want to find one that I'm serious about. I respect women much more than that. I'm like, you know what? It's okay for musicians not to be womanizers."

To Aiken, scoring one-night stands with groupies holds no appeal, because "that's all you're getting. And for the rock star, whoever it is, it's just as horrible for them. I'm not interested in trying to find seventeen different girls for every city I'm in. That's just stupid."

In any event, Clay has said, his life is too busy for a relationship. But if he did have the time, his idea of the perfect date might seem dull to some. "I'm pretty quiet. I like simplicity, like dinner and a movie—and that can either be at the house, or a movie theater. I don't think I'm a romantic really. I'm kind of spontaneous. Maybe that is romantic."

He values trustworthiness over almost everything and finds independence appealing. "You can't overlook looks, but to me independence is sexy. My mom is a very strong and independent person. She's prissy and all, but she's independent and she's strong—strong-minded and strong-willed. I think I want someone who's kind of like my mom." Clay says he does believe there is someone out there meant for him. "Hopefully, there's more than one, because if I mess up that first time, I hope there's a second."

In February 2004, newspapers around the country reported that Vernon Grissom had died at Franklin Regional Hospital in Louisburg at the age of sixty-eight. As fate would have it, Clay was performing in Raleigh on the very day of Grissom's funeral, which was held at Bright Funeral Home. Grissom was then buried at Woodland Baptist Church cemetery. Clay did not attend.

Perhaps the saddest consequence of Vernon's death was that there would always be unresolved issues for Clay, whether he realized it or not. During his interview with Diane Sawyer, Clay revealed that he still had some emotional ties with his birth father. When Sawyer asked, "If your dad called you on the phone, would you talk with him?" Clay said he would. Then she asked what it was Clay would like to hear Vernon say. Clay answered, "'I love you'—and mean it." Grissom died without ever picking up the phone.

As for the future, it appears it'll be whatever Clay chooses. His tour went well, and his first album sold over 3 million copies in the first year. Even so, Simon Cowell said, "It's too early to know which of the *Idol* alumni will be long-term superstars [because] *American Idol* and all the other *Idol* shows have been one big experiment. But I do think that Clay Aiken is the best thing to happen to *American Idol.* He changed the competition. He wasn't what anyone expected in a pop star, he epitomized the American dream and his makeover was like something out of a Hollywood movie."

In his book, *I Don't Mean to Be Rude, But . . . ,* Cowell elaborated further. "Clay . . . proved the point—you don't need to look like a male model to triumph in a contest like ours. Talent, personality, and determination will get you through.

"I confess that during season one I had my own ideas about what the American Idol should look like. It wasn't Clay Aiken. I have always trusted the general public, and when we said, 'What do you want?' in season two, they told us: 'Talent! Not hype.' He is one of the best things to ever happen to *American Idol*—he broke the mold.

"But Clay's success wasn't a fluke. . . . I think Clay can do whatever he wants in the future: sell records, act, or headline Vegas. I saw him two months after *American Idol* finished. He hadn't changed. Thank God."

And if Clay has anything to say about it, he won't. That's why he still hasn't taken off the WWJD (What Would Jesus Do) bracelet that was a gift one of his former YMCA summer campers sent him during the *Idol* competition. "It has more significance now than ever," Clay said thoughtfully. "It reminds me of who put me here. It reminds me that I can trust God, who had a different plan for me. It reminds me that I want to be a role model. And it reminds me that when he's ready for me to be done with this, this ride's gonna be over."

Quick Facts

Birth Date: November 30, 1978
Shares Birthday with: Dick Clark, Mark Twain, and Winston Churchill
Full Name: Clayton Holmes (Grissom) Aiken
Nicknames: Clay, Gonzo
Height: 6′ 1″
Weight: 145
Eyes: Hazel
Hair: Naturally red
Shoe Size: 12
Hometown: Raleigh, North Carolina
Mother: Faye Aiken Parker
Biological Father: Vernon Grissom (deceased)
Father: Ray Parker (deceased)
Stepsister: Amy
Stepbrother: Jeff
Half brother: Brett
Half sister: Deborah Grissom (deceased)
Education: Graduate of UNC–Charlotte with a degree in special education
Religion: Southern Baptist
His Idol: "My mother is the strongest person I know."
Life Goals: "Success, happiness, stability. I would love to be known as a generous and selfless person."
Phobias: Water
Favorite Movies: Comedies
Favorite Foods: Macaroni and cheese, Krispy Kreme donuts
Favorite Snack: Bi-Lo peanut butter cookies
Favorite Drink: Coke
Favorite Pizza Topping: Pepperoni
Favorite Song to Sing: "Unchained Melody"
Chinese Zodiac Sign: Horse
Favorite Pastimes: Watching movies, spending time with family and friends

Hidden Talent: He can turn both his feet around backward
Trademark: His wink
Favorite Female Pop Artists: Shania Twain and Faith Hill
Favorite Male Pop Artists: Jon Secada and Peter Cetera
Favorite Album: James Taylor's *Hourglass*
Favorite Song to Sing: "Unchained Melody"
Favorite Video Game: *Dead or Alive 3*
Pets: Raleigh, a border terrier
Allergies: Chocolate, coffee, mint, shellfish, almonds, and mushrooms

Discography

Album
Measure of a Man (2003)
Tracks:
"Invisible"
"I Will Carry You"
"The Way"
"When You Say You Love Me"
"No More Sad Songs"
"Run to Me"
"Shine"
"I Survived You"
"This Is the Night" (bonus cut)
"Perfect Day"
"Measure of a Man"
"Touch"

Singles
"Bridge Over Troubled Water" / "This Is the Night" (2003)
"Invisible" (2003)
"Measure of a Man" (2003)
"Solitaire" (2004)

American Idol Recordings

Collections
American Idol Season 2: All Time Classic American Love Songs (2003)
American Idol: The Great Holiday Classics (2003)

Singles
"What the World Needs Now" (2003)
"God Bless the U.S.A." (2003)

Writing by Clay Aiken

Learning to Sing: Hearing the Music in Your Life, with Allison Glock (2004)
Foreword to *Yes, Your Parents Are Crazy! A Teen Survival Handbook,* by Michael J. Bradley

Television Appearances

Variety/Specials
2004
A Capitol Fourth
AFI's 100 Years . . . 100 Songs
2003
31st Annual American Music Awards
Fromage 2003
The Nick at Night Holiday Special
An American Idol Christmas
Miss America Pageant
2002
American Idol: Search for a Superstar

Talk Show Guest Appearances
Gimme the Mike—June 2, 2004 (Premiere Episode)
The Tonight Show with Jay Leno—May 11, 2004
Saturday Night Live—February 7, 2004
The Tonight Show with Jay Leno—January 22, 2004
Celebrities Uncensored—November 26, 2003
Total Request Live—November 25, 2003
The Late Show with David Letterman—November 24, 2003
Jimmy Kimmel Live—November 13, 2003
Ellen: The Ellen DeGeneres Show—November 6, 2003
The Wayne Brady Show—October 28, 2003
The Early Show—October 17, 2003
The View—October 17, 2003

Good Morning America—October 15, 2003
The Tonight Show with Jay Leno—October 13, 2003
Primetime Live—October 9, 2003

Episodic
Ed—playing himself in "Pressure Points" episode, January 23, 2004

Awards
November 2003 Fans' Choice Award—American Music Awards
December 2003 Best-Selling Single of the Year—*Billboard* Award for debut single, "This Is the Night"

Clay's Complete *American Idol* Song List

"Over the Rainbow"—October 14, 2002 (Raleigh tryout)
"Perfect Strangers" / "Always and Forever"—October 21, 2002 (Atlanta tryout)
"Open Arms"—February 11, 2003
"Don't Let the Sun Go Down On Me"—March 4, 2003
"I Can't Help Myself"—March 11, 2003
"Somewhere Out There"—March 18, 2003
"Someone Else's Star"—March 25, 2003
"Everlasting Love"—April 1, 2003
"At This Moment"—April 8, 2003
"Tell Her About It"—April 15, 2003
"I Could Not Ask For More"—April 22, 2003
"Build Me Up Buttercup" / "Solitaire"—April 29, 2003
"To Love Somebody" / "Grease"—May 6, 2003
"Vincent" / "Mack The Knife" / "Unchained Melody"—May 13, 2003
"This Is the Night" / "Here, There and Everywhere" / "Bridge Over Troubled Water"—May 20, 2003

American Idol 2 Finalist's Individual Performances

March 11
Ruben: "Baby I Need Your Lovin'"
Clay: "I Can't Help Myself"
Kimberley: "Heat Wave"
Joshua: "Baby I Need Your Lovin'"
Trenyce: "Come See About Me"
Carmen: "You Can't Hurry Love"
Kimberly C.: "Nowhere To Run"

Rickey: "ABC"
Corey: "This Old Heart of Mine"
Julia: "Where Did Our Love Go?"
Charles: "How Sweet It Is"
Vanessa: "You Keep Me Hanging On"

March 18
Ruben: "A Whole New World"
Clay: "Somewhere Out There"
Kimberley: "Home"
Joshua: "I Don't Want To Miss A Thing"
Trenyce: "I Have Nothing"
Carmen: "Hopelessly Devoted To You"
Kimberly C.: "Shoop Shoop Song"
Rickey: "It Might Be You"
Corey: "Against All Odds"
Julia: "Flashdance! (What a Feeling)"
Charles: "You Can Win"

March 25
Ruben: "Sweet Home Alabama"
Clay: "Someone Else's Star"
Kimberley: "I Can't Make You Love Me"
Joshua: "Ain't Goin' Down 'Til the Sun Comes Up"
Trenyce: "I Need You"
Carmen: "Wild Angels"
Kimberly C.: "Anymore"
Rickey: "I've Done Enough Dyin' Today"
Corey: "Drift Away"
Julia DeMato: "Breathe"

April 1
Ruben: "Can't Get Enough of Your Love"
Clay: "Everlasting Love"
Kimberley: "It's Raining Men"
Joshua: "Celebration"

Trenyce: "I'm Every Woman"
Carmen: "Turn the Beat Around"
Kimberly C.: "Knock On Wood"
Rickey: "Let's Groove Tonight"

April 8
Ruben: "Kiss and Say Goodbye"
Clay: "At This Moment"
Kimberley: "My Heart Will Go On"
Joshua: "Amazed"
Trenyce: "The Power of Love"
Carmen: "Call Me"
Kimberly C.: "(Everything I Do) I Do It for You"
Rickey: "Endless Love"

April 15
Ruben: "Just the Way You Are"
Clay: "Tell Her About It"
Kimberley: "New York State of Mind"
Joshua: "Piano Man"
Trenyce: "Baby Grand"
Carmen: "And So It Goes"
Kimberly C.: "It's Still Rock 'n Roll to Me"

April 22
Ruben: "Music of My Heart"
Clay: "I Could Not Ask For More"
Kimberley: "If You Asked Me To"
Joshua: "That's When I'll Stop Loving You"
Trenyce: "Have You Ever?"
Carmen: "Love Will Lead You Back"

April 29
Ruben: "Breaking Up Is Hard To Do" / "Ain't Too Proud to Beg"
Clay: "Solitaire" / "Build Me Up Buttercup"
Kimberley: "Where the Boys Are" / "I Heard It Through the Grapevine"
Joshua: "Bad Blood" / "Then You Can Tell Me Goodbye"
Trenyce: "Love Will Keep Us Together" / "Proud Mary"

May 6
Ruben: "How Can You Mend a Broken Heart" / "Nights on Broadway"
Clay: "To Love Somebody" / "Grease"
Kimberley: "Emotion" / "I Just Want To Be Your Everything"
Joshua: "To Love Somebody"/ "Jive Talkin'"

May 13
Ruben: "Signed, Sealed, Delivered" / "Smile" / "If Ever You're In My Arms Again"
Clay: "Vincent" / "Mack The Knife" / "Unchained Melody"
Kimberley: "Band of Gold" / "Anyone Who Had a Heart" / "Inseparable"

May 20
Ruben: "A House Is Not a Home" / "Imagine" / "Flying Without Wings
Clay: "This Is the Night" / "Here, There and Everywhere" / "Bridge Over Troubled Water"

Did You Know?

Quiana Parler, the twenty-three-year-old singer from Charleston who beat out Clay at the Raleigh tryouts, was among the 234 contestants who got to go to Hollywood, but she was cut before producers narrowed the field to the final 32 contestants. Two years later, Clay remembered Quiana and hired her to be one of his backup singers for his solo tour. During the act, she joined Clay for a duet of "Without You."

On June 19, 2003, former *American Idol* finalist Corey Clark pleaded no contest to the charge of "obstruction of legal process" as part of a plea agreement reached with the Topeka District Attorney. According to the Smoking Gun Web site, he "was sentenced to six months unsupervised probation and ordered to pay $116 in court costs. Two other misdemeanor counts were dropped as part of the plea agreement."

Each *American Idol* finalist was given free cell phone usage by one of the show's sponsors. Ruben programmed his ring to play the Sean Paul song "Get Busy," while Clay went for the *American Idol* theme song.

Malcolm in the Middle star Frankie Muniz found himself in an awkward position at the Hollywood premiere of *X2*. Muniz, who had appeared with Clay in a local theater production of *The Sound of Music* six years earlier, had previously announced his support for Ruben. But at the premiere, he declared himself an Aiken fan. Frankie later admitted he didn't remember having acted with Clay until he saw him at the premiere.

"Den mother" Paula Abdul would give the finalists charms. Clay wore his on a braided leather chain. They included: "Sing your heart out as if no one's listening."

"Dance like a fool as if no one's watching."
"Good luck with your wishbone—you'll still need a backbone."
"Be who you are—be that completely. Find your inner peace."

Clay prompted some creative sign making, such as Clay Is Adorkable.

Clay had taken to heart the judges' comments in Atlanta about his appearance, so before leaving for the L.A. callbacks, he decided to dye his hair brown. A friend of Faye's offered to help, but the results were not exactly what Clay had in mind. "She actually dyed my hair blue first. I looked just like an old lady." Clay eventually got the color right, and when he moved on to the final twelve, Clay had his teeth whitened and bonded.

Aiken says one of his worst habits is correcting people's grammar. "I hate it when people use double plurals or double negatives. That's my big one." He is also a stickler for promptness. "If one person tells me to be somewhere at six P.M. and I show up and they're not there, or it doesn't happen at all . . . I'm reasonable, but if you say you are gonna be there, you need to be there."

Clay's idea of a good time is goofing off with friends, playing board games such as Taboo or playing hide and seek. "The reason kids have more fun than anyone else is because they don't care what anyone thinks of them, and that's my goal—not to care what anyone thinks!"

For the 2004 North Carolina State Fair, Clay was paid $100,000 to perform, making him the highest paid entertainer in fair history.

Had Clay not found success as a performer, his plan after college graduation was to teach for six years, then attend the College of William and Mary for a master's degree in administration. Even now he says, "I still would love to. I could still see myself as a school principal at the age of fifty."

Ruben Studdard's lawsuit against 205 Flava was settled in December 2003. Although the exact terms were confidential, it was announced that 19 Entertainment, Simon Fuller's UK-based company that owns all the *Idol* series, would begin marketing 205 Flava products. Both sides appeared satisfied, especially the owners of 205 Flava, since 19 Entertainment will be able to market and license the clothing line internationally.

Prior to *Pop Idol* and *American Idol,* British music producer Simon Fuller was best known as the man who managed the Spice Girls.

The National League of Junior Cotillions named Clay Aiken the Best Mannered Person of 2003, honoring "his example of humility and politeness." Second on the list was Oprah Winfrey. Anne Colvin Winters, the league's executive director, said, "Clay Aiken of *American Idol* fame was chosen because of the courteous manner in which he treats fellow performers and fans." Rounding out the Top Ten list were General Tommy Franks, first lady Laura Bush, Atlanta Falcons quarterback Michael Vick, actor Mel Gibson, surfer Bethany Hamilton, NBC news anchor PERLINK "http://entertainment.msn.com/celebs/celeb.aspx?c=327935" Tom Brokaw, National Security Adviser Condoleezza Rice, and British Prime Minister Tony Blair. Previous Best Mannered winners have included Microsoft founder Bill Gates and baseball player Mark McGwire.

What is the secret to Clay's spiky hairstyle? Dippity-do Techno-Style Stretch Putty.

Although he doesn't mind hearing his records, Clay admitted to *People* that he avoids hearing himself talk whenever possible. "To listen to myself talk makes me cringe. I don't even like to hear myself on an answering machine." It's ironic then that Clay agreed to narrate some audio versions for the Arthur Adventure Series children's books. "I don't think kids would recognize my voice unless I sang the book. They're going to say, 'Mama, who is this kid with this country accent?' Most moms will recognize me, only because I sound like such a big hick."

Did you know that Clay prefers his yogurt to have the fruit on the bottom? You can learn other likes and dislikes by reading the contract rider for his current tour at http://www.thesmokinggun.com/backstagetour/clay/clay1.html.

About the Author

Kathleen Tracy has been an entertainment journalist for over twenty years. Her writing has been featured in magazines including *Film News International, A&E Biography* Magazine, *KidScreen, Video Age* and *TV Times*. She is also the author of over 20 books including the biographies "The Boy Who Would Be King"(Dutton), "Jerry Seinfeld: The Entire Domain" (Carol Publishing), "Angelina Jolie" (ECW), "Don Imus: America's Cowboy" (Carroll & Graf) and most recently "Diana Rigg: The Biography" from Benbella Books. She has also written the companions "The Girl's Got Bite: A Guide to Buffy's World" (St. Martin's Press) and "The Complete Jackie Chan Handbook" (Simon & Schuster).